AN ILLUSTRATED GUIDE TO
STRATEGIC
WEAPONS

D1067776

AN ILLUSTRATED GUIDE TO
STRATEGIC
WEAPONS

Max Walmer

PRENTICE HALL PRESS
New York   London   Toronto   Sydney   Tokyo

A Salamander Book

Prentice Hall Press
Gulf + Western Building
One Gulf + Western Plaza
New York, New York   10023

355.8
WAL

An Arco Military Book

Published by the Prentice Hall Trade Division

PRENTICE HALL PRESS and colophon are registered
trademarks of Simon & Schuster Inc.

Originally published in 1988 in the United Kingdom by
Salamander Books Ltd., 52 Bedford Row, London WC1R 4LR.

This book may not be sold outside the United States
of America and Canada.

Library of Congress Cataloging-in-Publication Data

Walmer, Max
  An Illustrated guide to strategic weapons.
  (An Arco military book)
  1. Nuclear weapons. 2. Nuclear weapons — Pictorial
works. 1. Title. II. Series.
U264.M548 1988   355.8'25119   87-47991
ISBN 0-13-451071-2

10 9 8 7 6 5 4 3 2 1

First Prentice Hall Press Edition

Credits

Author: Max Walmer has contributed numerous articles to technical
defence journals on subjects ranging from guerilla warfare to missile
strategy. His work includes "An Illustrated Guide to Modern Elite Forces".

Managing Editor: Ray Bonds
Editor: Ashley Brown
Designed by: James Daniels Ltd.
Diagrams: TIGA
Filmset by The Old Mill
Color reproduction by Rodney Howe Ltd.
Printed in Belgium by Proost International Book Production, Turnhout.

Photographs: The publishers wish to thank all the official governmental
archives, aircraft and system manufacturers, and private individuals, who
have supplied photographs for this book.

Contents

Missile and Warhead Technology

Ballistic Missiles

There are two types of strategic ballistic missile: land-based ICBMs and submarine-based SLBMs. Both of these types of missile consist of three elements: the power unit, the payload and a guidance system. The power unit consists of 'stages', each of which is a fuel storage container with one or more rocket motors at its base, these stages being shed progressively during the flight as their fuel is used up. The payload is contained at the front of the missile, and consists of re-entry vehicles (RVs) and other items such as penetration aids and decoys. This 'front-end' may include a post-boost vehicle (which is virtually a fourth stage), containing the 'bus', on which the re-entry vehicles (RVs) are mounted and inside which are the nuclear warheads covered by a 'shroud' or nose-cone. The third element is the guidance package, which controls the missile during the flight.

The missiles are propelled by rocket motors, powered by either liquid or solid fuels. First-generation missiles of the 1950s and 1960s invariably used liquid fuels, which were difficult to store in the missile itself. Propellants such as liquid oxygen offer excellent performance, but are not only difficult to store; they are also not easy to feed into a missile during a rapid count-down, an important limitation when under attack. For the second generation missiles, both ICBM and SLBM, the USSR adopted storable liquids, such as N_2O_4/UDMH, but the US followed this course only in the Titan II, which

used N_2O_4 and Aerozine 50. In the US Titan system, Titan I used very sophisticated 'super-rapid' loading devices for its liquid fuel, but still had a minimum reaction time of 20 minutes, whereas Titan II, which used storable liquids had a reaction time of just 60 seconds.

Solid-propellant rocket motors are simpler to construct than liquid-propellant motors, are easier and safer to store and maintain, and do not require time-consuming and dangerous on-site fuelling. Not everything is straightforward, however. The major problem with solid-fuel propulsion is that thrust cannot be controlled or terminated on command as is possible with liquid-fuel systems, and this has serious consequences for guiding the missile. This problem has been resolved, in various complex ways: in the US Peacekeeper, for example, the three main stages are solid-fuelled, but the

Right: The first US ICBM to be launched from a silo, Titan II had protection hardened to 300psi (21kg/cm²).

final stage (the 'deployment stage') is liquid-fuelled. This deployment stage uses a liquid, bi-propellant, axially-mounted rocket motor, which is able to provide velocity changes, while eight small engines provide attitude control. All US and other Western missiles and most Soviet missiles now use solid fuel in their main stages.

Missiles in Flight

Virtually all modern missiles are navigated and guided to their destinations by inertial guidance, a completely self-contained system that requires no external inputs once the missile has been launched. A few, however, do take external inputs: the US Peacekeeper missile takes updates from the Navstar satellite system.

Inertial guidance systems use Newton's Law, which relates the acceleration imparted to a body of cer-tain mass by an external force to determine the missile's path — in effect, this means that it measures the missile's path to determine its position and velocity, calculates the velocity the missile needs to reach the target, using a model of the forces the missile will experience after thrust termination, and then directs the rocket thrust to match that velocity. When the missile is in the required position, travelling at the correct velocity, the motor is closed down and the missile enters the free-flight phase.

A ballistic missile is only actually guided during the period of its rocket-burn (a few minutes at most) and the only variable that can be controlled in a solid-fuel motor is the direction of the thrust generated by the booster rocket. As the missile is accelerating in three dimensions, three accel-erometers are used, mounted or-thogonally (ie, mutually perpen-

Below: The US Atlas was mounted in a silo. The whole outfit was raised to the surface for launch.

dicular to each other) to measure the three components of the specific forces. These are themselves mounted on a gyroscopically-stabilised gimballed platform. The information from the accelerometers and gyroscopes is processed by the on-board computer, which calculates the velocity needed to reach the target from that position. It then takes the vector difference between the instantaneous current velocity and the required velocity and steers the rocket thrust parallel to that velocity.

Warheads

The first ballistic missiles had one warhead each. After the missile's final stage burnout, this warhead then separated onto a planned, unpowered trajectory which brought it to the target. As rocket motors became more powerful, these single warheads increased in yield as sheer brutal force was used to try to improve their chance of destroying a hardened target such as a missile silo. The US Titan II, for example, delivered a 9MT warhead with a CEP of 0.7nm (1.3km), while the Soviet SS-7 Mod 3 had a warhead with a yield of no less than 20-25MT, the largest practical yield it is worth deploying.

In the early 1960s US strategic planners deployed single warhead systems, but they found themselves faced with far more Soviet targets than they had missiles. One possible (albeit extremely expensive) solution would have been to build vast numbers of single-warhead missiles and silos, but they found the solution instead in the use of multiple re-entry vehicles, placing several warheads on one missile. This development was made feasible by the greater payload carrying capability of the missiles; the ever-improving yield: weight ratios of the nuclear warheads (that is, lighter warheads could deliver a greater explosive punch) and more sophisticated RV guidance systems.

At first, these warheads were, like shot from a hunting gun, all aimed at the same target and thus increased the 'chance' of a kill — these are termed Multiple Re-entry Vehicles

(MRVs). A variation of this was to aim such weapons at several targets, but all within the same very small area; the Soviet SS-9 Mod 4, for example, had three MRVs which impacted with the same spread as the three silos of a typical US Minuteman complex.

A number of missiles still in service are equipped with MRVs, but a new development has superseded them. Further technological advances enabled individual re-entry vehicles to be designed to follow independent paths to separate targets. This was

Peacekeeper MIRV and warheads.

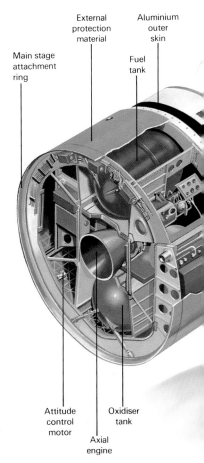

External protection material

Aluminium outer skin

Main stage attachment ring

Fuel tank

Attitude control motor

Oxidiser tank

Axial engine

done by mounting them on a 'bus', with tiny motors and a computer, as well as the RVs. Once the booster has brought the bus onto the correct general line for the target area the bus, controlled by its computer, uses its motors to bring it onto aim for the first target. Once this is correct the bus launches the RV and then adjusts its trajectory for the second target, discharges the next RV, adjusts its path for the third RV, and so on. This type of warhead is designated a Multiple Independently Targetable Re-entry Vehicle (MIRV). MIRV loads have increased from the three or four per missile, when they were first introduced, to loads of around ten today. Some missiles can even carry as many as 14. MIRVs are, like MRVs, unpowered and the distance by which the targets are separated is limited by the extra velocities the post-boost vehicle can impart. The 'footprint' of the six MIRVs on the French M4, for example, is an area of 192x81nm (350x150km).

The MIRV enables one missile to attack more than one target. This is of great significance not only to the

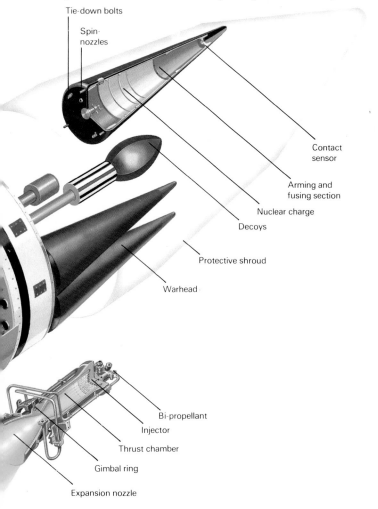

Tie-down bolts

Spin-nozzles

Contact sensor

Arming and fusing section

Nuclear charge

Decoys

Protective shroud

Warhead

Bi-propellant

Injector

Thrust chamber

Gimbal ring

Expansion nozzle

two Superpowers, but also to the lesser nuclear powers, such as China, France and the UK. A French SSBN, for example, armed with 16 single-warhead M20 missiles can attack 16 targets, whereas the same submarine armed with M4 missiles has the potential to attack a maximum of 96 targets. In practice, a proportion of targets would be attacked by two MIRVs to raise the probability of a 'kill'. Total targets attacked could, therefore, be somewhat less than 96 — but nevertheless, very considerably more than 16. It should be noted, however, that while MIRVs increase the number of targets which can be attacked, they limit the planners in other respects, in that the first RV automatically sets limits on the placing of the subsequent RVs and their time of arrival.

The warheads discussed so far all follow ballistic paths, which can be rapidly and accurately predicted by the defence. A further refinement, therefore, is to give each RV its own power-pack and the ability to steer itself. Designated the Manoeuvrable Re-entry Vehicle (MaRV), this device can carry out both high-level and terminal manoeuvres to confuse an enemy's detection and interception systems, while an on-board inertial system brings it back onto the target with an accuracy at least as good as a ballistic RV. The next step is the Precision-Guided Re-entry Vehicle (PGRV) in which terminal guidance is added to the MaRV, to bring it onto its designated target with an accuracy of tens of feet, or even less. Such accuracy would enable smaller warheads to achieve similar or even greater destructive power than larger warheads landing further away from the target; alternatively, a PGRV with a low-yield warhead could permit greater targeting flexibility with lower damage outside the immediate target area.

Radar observation can determine how many devices are launched by a missile bus by counting the number of course alterations, termed 'dips'. However, most missiles now carry decoys and devices known as 'penetration aids' (penaids) — for example, ECM devices, such as chaff and jammers — intended to confuse the defences. Decoys need to match the real RVs' radar signature (to mislead defending radars) and their thermal signature (to mislead infra-red detectors) — although it was suggested in a 1986 British TV programme that the British Chevaline system had adopted the opposite course, by making the real RVs look like decoys!

Throw Weight

Missile payload is termed 'throw weight' — in effect, the weight of warlike devices which can be lifted towards the target. It thus includes RVs, decoys and penaids, but excludes the bus and other parts of the missile itself.

Throw weight is obviously a function of the power of the missile's propulsion system and both have increased steadily over the years. The highest throw weights of their respective generations are possessed by the SS-11 (2,500lb — 1,134kg) and the SS-18 (16,700lb — 7,575kg). In all ballistic missiles the amount of fuel is fixed, so the only way to alter the range is by varying the payload. Range can be increased by reducing the number of RVs, penaids or decoys. RVs are becoming smaller and lighter, thus enabling more to be carried for the same weight, and both ICBM and SLBM missiles may well not be loaded to their theoretical capacity in order to achieve the range necessary for a specific target. A further factor is that certain targets may require more decoys or penaids than others. Again increases in these devices could only be met by reducing the number of RVs.

Precision

All modern missiles have the large warheads and precision of aim sufficient to destroy large area targets such as cities, industrial complexes or airfields. Greater precision only becomes necessary when the warhead is intended to destroy or damage pinpoint, hardened targets, such as ICBM silos or buried headquarters. The precision of such a warhead is expressed as the Circular Area Probable (CEP) which is the radius of a circle, centred upon the *mean point of impact*, that is the area

within which 50 percent of the warheads aimed at that target will fall. The size of the CEP is determined by a combination of theoretical study and empirical data obtained from the testing programme. The CEP is normally understood to apply to the missile's maximum range. When fired to less than range, the CEP reduces in the same proportion — so, a 5,000nm (9,260km) missile with a CEP of 0.5nm (0.93km), when fired to a range of 2,500nm (4,630km), will have a CEP of 0.5 x (2,500/5,000) = 0.25nm (0.47km).

Of great importance is the distance between the mean point of impact and the target itself; this is termed the *bias,* which is the cumulative effect of all system errors on the trajectory of the missile and the RV. For example, a critical component in a particular missile system, such as an accelerometer, might produce an error on operational trajectories such that the mean point of impact was 50ft (15m) beyond the centre of the target. Other more random events may affect the bias, such as the weather conditions over the target or uneven wear of the ablative shield during re-entry. Clearly, the requirement is for a warhead/missile system which has both a small CEP and small bias.

Lethal Radius

To destroy a 'hardened' target (defined as one protected against an overpressure exceeding 300psi (21.9kg/cm²)), a warhead must land close enough for the target to lie within its lethal radius. This lethal radius is a combination of various factors, the more important of which are the warhead yield, the hardness of the target and the density of the soil or rock within which the target is situated. Disregarding the nature of the soil, a 0.5MT warhead, aimed at a 2,000psi (146km/cm²) target, would have a lethal radius of approximately 0.136nm (250m).

Single-Shot Kill Probability

The Single-Shot Kill Probability (SSKP) is an expression of the probability that one warhead of specified

Below: In the 1980s ICBMs tended to be mobile- rather than silo-based. These non-strategic SS-20s follow this trend.

reliability will destroy a silo and is expressed either as a decimal (eg, 0.65) or as a percentage (eg, 65 percent). Thus, for example, a warhead with a 0.5MT yield, a CEP of 0.14nm (260m) and a reliability of 85 percent, attacking a target capable of withstanding an overpressure of 2,000psi (146kg/cm²) would have an SSKP of 0.54 (54 percent). If for the same warhead, the CEP was to be reduced to 0.1nm (185m) (in other words, if more missiles would be likely to be targeted accurately onto a smaller area), the SSKP would rise to 0.80 (80 percent). Calculations of lethal radii and SSKP are derived from *Nuclear Vulnerability Handbook,* by Ian Bellany, Centre for the Study of Arms Control and International Security, University of Lancaster, 1981.

ICBM Launch Techniques

There are two techniques for launching ICBMs from their silos: 'hot' and 'cold'. In the first 'hot' systems the missile was launched from the surface, having been raised by an elevator, but then missiles were launched from inside the silo by leading away the rocket motor exhaust, through ducts. This is no longer used, however, and all current 'hot' systems allow the rocket exhaust to flow up past the missile body as it lifts off, which gives a self-contained and simple system, but leads to considerable damage to the silo. Thus, it prevents re-use of the silo and is one of the main reasons why operational silos are not used for live, practice firings in peacetime.

The USSR, however, has successfully pioneered the 'cold' launch

technqiue which was developed originally for use in SSBNs. In this the missile is ejected clear of the silo by high-pressure gas, its first-stage motor only firing when well clear of the silo. This means that the silo can be re-used after a short period; it also means that a larger missile can be used in an existing silo, since it is no longer necessary to restrict the diameter of the missile body to allow the rocket exhaust to flow up past it.

ICBM Launch Silos

The first operational ballistic missile system, the German A-4 (V-2) was a small, single-warhead system, which, because of the air threat to fixed launch sites, was fired from a land-mobile launcher. From this were developed ever-larger ICBM systems carrying an ever-increasing number of RVs and based in increasingly sophisticated silos. Nowadays, the wheel has come full circle: because of the air threat (albeit this time from missiles rather than from aircraft) development is concentrating on small, single-warhead systems, fired from land-mobile launchers.

ICBM silos are very complicated underground launch centres, normally sited at relatively high altitude to increase the missiles' range, and in springy ground to absorb as much as possible of the impact from the detonation of incoming warheads. (Rocky ground provides much less shock insulation.) Essentially a vertical, reinforced-concrete tube, a silo accommodates an elaborate suspension and isolation system, which not only supports the missile, but also provides yet further shock protection, minimizing the transfer of motion from the walls and floor of the silo to the missile. The top third of the silo is surrounded by a multi-storey structure housing the maintenance and launch facilities. The whole is capped by a massive sliding door, which is designed to provide protection against overpressure by transmitting the shock to the cover supports rather than to the vertical tube containing the missile. The sliding door also provides protection against the radiation effects of attacking nuclear warheads and sweeps away debris as it opens, to prevent it from falling into the missile tube and possibly interfering with the launch process.

Silos are grouped into launch complexes comprising a number of silos sited sufficiently far apart to ensure that one incoming warhead cannot destroy more than one missile. The complex is controlled by a command centre, which may be up to 100ft (30m) underground. US practice is to control ten silos from one launch centre; a French S-3 command centre controls nine silos. One of the major vulnerabilities is the communications, power and systems monitoring cabling between the command cen-

Left: Closely Spaced Basing, proposed for the US MX ICBM, would have had 100 silos some 1,800ft (550m) apart.

tre and the silos, which may be affected by blast or, in particular, by Electro-Magnetic Pulse (EMP). Elaborate measures are taken to minimise the possibility of such damage and the USA, for example, has completed two programmes in this area at the Minuteman silos (the Hardened Intersite Cable System (HICS) and the Minuteman Extended Survival Power System (MESPS)), both designed to enhance survivability under attack.

The protection factor or 'hardness' of a silo is measured in its ability to withstand the overpressure resulting from the blast effects of a nuclear explosion. It is expressed in pounds-per-square-inch (psi) or kilo-grammes-per-square-centimetre (kg/cm^2) ($1psi = 0.073kg/cm^2$). In the USA the Titan II silos, constructed in the late 1950s, had a hardness of 300psi ($22kg/cm^2$), while Minuteman silos (mid-1960s) were built with a hardness of some 1,200psi ($88kg/cm^2$). All current silos for both Minuteman III and Peacekeeper are of approximately 2,000psi ($146kg/cm^2$) and Congress has refused repeated requests to increase this. It is reported that there has been a large-scale hardening programme in the USSR, silos housing SS-18, for example, being hardened to withstand an overpressure of 5,000psi ($365kg/cm^2$).

Other factors are, of course, involved. The probability that a missile silo will fail is more closely related to the impulse (the overpressure integrated over time) than simply to the peak overpressure. Further, the effectiveness of a specific detonation depends upon the nature of the ground in which the silo is located and the current state of the local water-table.

Strategic Missile Submarines

A ballistic missile submarine (SSBN) is essentially a collection of missile launching tubes, but one which has a fundamental advantage over the land-based silos in that it is able to

Right: SLBMs introduced a new dimension to strategic warfare as their SSBN launch platforms can hide deep in the sea.

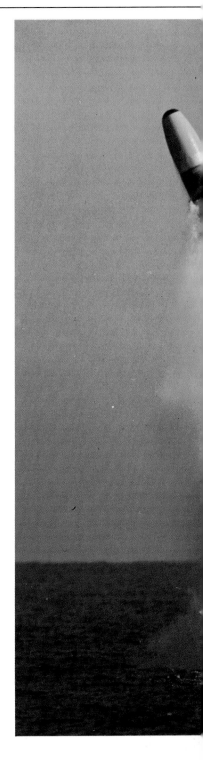

hide in the vastness of the ocean. Modern SSBNs have at least 12 missiles, most have 16 and the latest have either 20 or 24, all arranged vertically and abaft the fin, except for the Soviet Typhoon class in which the tubes are before the fin. SSBNs usually make fairly fast transits from their home port to their operational area, where they then cruise at about 2-3knots (3.8-5.6km/hr), varying their depth to take maximum advantage of oceanic conditions to make detection as difficult as possible. All modern SSBNs are capable of launching their SLBMs from below the surface, as well as while surfaced. A gas-generator is used to blow the missile out of its launch tube and up towards the surface, where the first-stage motor ignites, and it then follows a mission profile similar to that of an ICBM. The Soviet Typhoon and Delta IV class SSBNs can, in addition to underwater launching, surface in the ice of the Arctic and fire from there.

Until very recently all SSBNs launched their SLBMs one after the other. Known firing rates are one missile every 50 seconds for a US Poseidon boat and one missile every 55 seconds for a French Le Redoutable boat. However, a Soviet

Below: US Trident I C-4 SLBMs are loaded in their launch canisters into the missile tubes of an Ohio class SSBN.

Typhoon is known to have carried out successful tests firing pairs of SS-N-20s in salvo.

The Effects Of Nuclear Weapons

The advent of nuclear weapons and the prospect of their use permeates every aspect of general war planning in all major nations. There is clearly a possibility that the use of strategic nuclear weapons could accomplish either, at one end of the scale, the total elimination of large elements of the engaged nations (and probably of many nations not directly involved in the conflict, as well) or, at the other, the precision destruction of critical point targets, such as ICBM silos, airfields, headquarters, communica-

tions centres and logistic bases.

Nuclear weapons have never been used, and atomic weapons only twice — at Hiroshima and Nagasaki in the closing days of World War Two, but these two attacks have given frightening examples of the power of modern strategic forces. The immediate effects of nuclear explosions are blast, thermal radiation, electromagnetic pulse (EMP), and initial radiation. The magnitude of these effects depends upon the height of the burst above the ground and its explosive power, or 'yield'. This 'yield' is a measure of the strength of the energy the nuclear weapon produces and is usually stated in terms of the quantity of conventional explosive (TNT) which

would generate the same amount of explosive energy. The two bombs dropped on Japan, for example, had a nominal yield of 20 kilotons (20KT): that is, they were equivalent to 20,000 tons of TNT. The largest known test was of a bomb with a yield of 70MT (equivalent to 70 million tons of TNT), carried out by the USSR in the 1960s.

In general terms the energy produced by a nuclear explosion can be divided into three categories: kinetic energy (the energy motion of electrons, molecules and atoms as a whole); the internal energy of these particles; and thermal radiation energy. For a nuclear explosion in the atmosphere below an altitude of about 100,000ft (30,480m) some 35 to 45 percent of the explosion energy is received as thermal energy in the visible and infra-red portions of the spectrum; while below an altitude of 40,000ft (12,000m) about 50 percent of the explosive energy is used in producing air shock, 35 percent of the remainder producing thermal radiation.

The thermal effects are caused by the extreme intensity of the flash of the explosion and its heat — over 100,000 degrees Centigrade. The effects of the flash depend on the power of the weapon and of the general conditions — whether the explosion occurs by day or by night, its duration, the weather conditions and the general terrain. The physical effects of heat and light on people and equipment outside the immediate area of the explosion can be predicted from tables derived from actual nuclear tests.

Radiation has both immediate and long-term effects. With smaller devices (up to about 20KT airburst) only about 15 percent of the overall casualties would be caused by radiation. Repeated exposures to radiation do, however, have a cumulative effect. Residual radiation results mainly from fallout, the dust cloud spreading after the explosion. Militarily, residual radiation can deny an enemy either transit through or use of a contaminated area.

There has been considerable controversy over the 'Enhanced Radiation' weapon, popularly described as the 'Neutron Bomb'. This is a thermonuclear device designed to maximize the lethal effects of high energy neutrons and to reduce the blast effect. The result is that, for a given yield, a lethal dose of nuclear radiation is delivered over a greater area than for a fission bomb. The consequence is that people suffer from the radiation effects, while the physical damage to buildings, vehicles and equipment is much reduced. It should be noted, however, that ER weapons are of 1KT yield or less, since it is only in such small yields that the radiation-kill radius exceeds the destructive effects of the same weapon due to blast. It is highly improbable that an ER weapon would be used in a strategic role, except possibly in the warhead of an ABM.

The principal electromagnetic effect resulting from a nuclear explosion is the electromagnetic pulse (EMP), which can damage electronic and electrical equipment having insufficient protection against this sudden, massive, albeit very shortlived, pulse of electromagnetic energy. EMP can affect telecommunications equipment and long cabling, such as overhead telephone wires and power cables (where these still exist), as well as disrupting radio communications, although the actual effects depend to a great extent on the height and yield of the nuclear explosion and on the design and nature of the electronic/electrical equipment. A well-authenticated example of EMP occurred during nuclear tests in 1962 when thirty 'strings' (series-connected loops) of street lights at various locations on the Hawaiian island of Oahu failed simultaneously as a result of a high-altitude airburst over Johnson Island, some 700nm (1,300km) distant. In a strategic exchange, much military equipment could be degraded, if not actually destroyed, causing command, control and communications to be, at the very least, seriously disrupted. A, burst at about 70,000ft (21,300m) over the centre of the USA, for example, would have a devastating effect

Right: Eight MIRVs from a USAF Peacekeeper ICBM head towards impact on the Kwajalein range in the South Pacific.

on US strategic control just at the time it was most urgently required.

For many years nuclear weapons had a fixed yield. Later, warheads were designed with yields which could be altered between three or four settings while on the ground in a lengthy and laborious process. Today's weapons, however, have variable yields which can be selected easily and rapidly on the receipt of fire orders. A pilot can do it in flight.

Warheads also contain safety and control devices designed to prevent unauthorised, accidental or inadvertent use. All modern US weapons include a Permissive Action Link (PAL), a locking device in the arming system, which requires the insertion of a code to unlock the circuits to arm the weapon. Most recent versions of PAL will render the control system unusable if incorrect numbers are repeatedly inserted (this is known as a 'limited try' facility). In addition, the latest mobile weapons, which need to be transported frequently, also contain 'insensitive high explosives' (IHE) which are more resistant to detonation by fire, small arms, aircraft crash or accidental release in flight.

Minuteman II (LGM-30F)

Status: In service
Dimensions: Length 57ft 6in (17.53m); diameter 72.4in (184cm)
Range: 6,750nm (12,500km)
Launch weight: 73,000lb (33,112kg)
Throw weight: 1,600lb (726kg)
Propulsion: Three-stage; solid-fuel; hot launch
Guidance: Inertial gimballed NS-17 guidance and control system
Warhead: One W-56 warhead; Mark 11C re-entry vehicle; 1.2MT
CEP: 0.16nm (370m)

Development: Minuteman I was the first solid-fuel ICBM to become operational. All previous missiles had been liquid fuelled. Development started in 1956 on an IRBM, but in 1957 it was realised that intercontinental range would be feasible and the project was upgraded to ICBM status. Virtually every part of the programme broke new ground: propulsion, guidance, construction, launching and siting. The three stages were given to different companies to develop: 1st stage — Thiokol, 2nd stage — Aerojet, 3rd stage — Hercules. The first missile flew on time on February 1, 1961. Deployment in silos began in December 1962 and 800 silos were at full operational readiness by June 1965.

Progressive development led to Minuteman II, the first of which flew in September 1964. This was longer and heavier than the earlier Minuteman I — a new 2nd stage motor gave increased range. A new guidance system was also fitted, together with a micro-electronic memory storing data for numerous targets. The whole package gave greater accuracy over greater ranges. The AVCO Mark IIB or C RV has a 1.2MT warhead and Tracor Mark I or 1A penaids, the first to be fitted to a US missile. IOC was achieved in 1966 and Minuteman II eventually totally replaced Minuteman I.

After long service, age began to tell. An improvement programme over the period FY 1984-89 to replace worn-out parts in the guidance system, coupled with general upgrading, resulted in an increase in accuracy of some 38 percent. Also, the Rivet Mile programme (see Minuteman III) upgraded the launch and control facilities.

Deployment: 450 Minuteman II are deployed, of which eight are configured for the Emergency Rocket Communications System (see below), all located at Whiteman Air Force Base. Full deployment has 150 missiles at Malstrom Air Force Base, 150 at Ellsworth Air Force Base and 142 plus the eight ERCS missiles at Whiteman Air Force Base.

Employment: Since the withdrawal of the last Titan II in 1987 Minuteman II is the only US ICBM with a large, single, high-yield warhead. This would enable

this missile to be used against moderately hard targets. It is also usable against soft, large-area, military and industrial installations requiring high yield but less than pinpoint accuracy, as well as isolated targets.

Eight targets are set in the missile computer, of which one is the default primary. Re-programming of the target data takes some 36 hours, which is clearly of little military value, but the Command Data Buffer System, which reduces repogramming time to just 25 minutes and is being installed in Minuteman III is not scheduled for Minuteman II.

The Emergency Rocket Communication System (ERCS) provides a 'last-ditch' strategic communications system, particularly to SSBNs. The Minuteman II missiles carry the radio equipment in place of the nuclear warheads and the system provides, in effect, a short-lived, sub-orbital communications satellite facility, either by acting as a rebroadcast station for messages or by broadcasting a message tape-recorded immediately before launch. Other rockets, not in the strategic inventory, would be used to replace space-based satellites destroyed by enemy action.

Minuteman II is clearly very vulnerable to a Soviet first strike and it is hardly a coincidence that the 'footprint' of the three MRVs in the SS-11 Mod 3 fits almost exactly the shape of a Minuteman II complex.

Below left: Simultaneous launch of two USAF Minuteman II ICBMs at Vandenburg AFB, Cal.

Below: Silo launch of Minuteman II ICBM from one of six SAC bases.

Minuteman III (LGM-30G)

Status: In service
Dimensions: Length 59ft 8.5in (18.2m); diameter 72.4in (184cm)
Range: 6,750nm (12,500km)
Launch weight: 76,058lb (34,500kg)
Throw weight: 2,400lb (1,088kg)
Propulsion: Three-stage; solid-fuel; hot launch
Guidance: All inertial, gimballed, Improved NS-20 system
Warhead: *Either* General Electric Mark 12 RV with three 170KT W-62 warheads, chaff and decoys (236 missiles); *or* General Electric Mark 12A RV with three 335KT W-78 MIRV warheads and decoys (300 missiles)
CEP: Mark 12 RV — 0.12nm (220m); Mark 12A RV — 0.09nm (166m)

Development: Minuteman III introduced a new third stage and was the first US ICBM with MIRVs. The third stage has a greater diameter than that of Minuteman II and a single fluid-injection nozzle. The Post Boost Propulsion System (PBPS) has a 300lb (136kg) motor for fore/aft thrusting, six 22lb (10kg) motors for yaw/pitch, and four skin-mounted 18lb (8kg) motors for roll. Early Minuteman IIIs carry the Mark 12As with three 350KT W-78 warheads and greatly improved CEP.

A programme to improve the accuracy of the Minuteman III was started in FY 1982 and completed in FY 1987. This has involved the identification of accuracy error sources in the missile computer hardware and software; there are

Below: Minuteman III was the first MIRV-equipped US ICBM.

Right: Minuteman IIIs, launched from Vandenburg AFB.

claims that this has led to a 25 percent improvement in accuracy. A further pro-gramme called Rivet Mile is modifying the existing Minuteman II and III launch and control facilities.

Deployment: There were originally 550 Minuteman III missiles deployed. However, the 50 Peacekeeper missiles are being deployed in erstwhile Minuteman III silos at Warren Air Force Base on a one-for-one basis and, as at December 31, 1987, the inventory of Minuteman III had been reduced by 14 as a result. Current deployment is, therefore, 536 missiles, with 50 at Malmstrom Air Force Base, 150 at Minot Air Force Base, 186 at Warren Air Force Base, and 150 at Grand Forks Air Force Base.

Employment: The 300 missiles with the 335KT W-78/Mark 12A RVs have suf-ficient combination of accuracy and yield to be targeted against most harden-ed targets, and it would be reasonable to assume that at least some of them are targeted against Soviet missile silos and command bunkers. The 236 missiles with Mark 12 RVs are, however, not quite so effective and are, no doubt, targeted against slightly less demanding hard targets.

Individual missile computers have a three-target selection capability for each of the three MIRVs, one set in each being designated default primary. The Command Data Buffer system, fitted from FY 1975 onwards, enables each missile to be retargeted on the ground in 25 minutes or the whole force to be retargeted in 10 hours. In addition, post-launch retargeting can be carried out from a Boeing E-4B airborne command post.

Peacekeeper (MGM-118A)

Status: In service
Dimensions: Length 71ft (21.6m); diameter 92in (233cm)
Range: 6,000nm (11,000km)
Launch weight: 193,000ib (87,500kg)
Throw weight: 7,000lb (3,175kg)
Propulsion: Four-stage; three solid-propellant booster motors; storable liquid hypergolic propellant in the fourth stage (post-boost vehicle); cold launch
Guidance: Inertial floating ball
Warhead: Mark 21 RV carrying 10 W-87 300KT warheads; maximum load is 12 warheads
CEP: 0.05nm (100m)

Above: Testing of the cold-launch technique for the USAF Peacekeeper ICBM.

Development: Like the B-1 strategic bomber the Peacekeeper (formerly MX) weapon system consumed money at a prodigious rate and gave rise to an enormous amount of controversy for many years without making any contribution to Western defence or deterrence. Though the need for a Minuteman replacement was self-evident, and there were no problems in producing the missile, arguments raged for many years on how to base it.

One idea was to use aircraft. In 1974 a packaged Minuteman was pulled by parachute from a Lockheed C-5 transport aircraft; the rocket motor ignited during the descent and the missile climbed away successfully. Then interest centred upon ground deployment, using road-mobile trucks or underground rail cars in buried tunnels; in the latter, the missile erector broke through the surface to enable launch to take place. The Carter Administration favoured such a Multiple Protective Shelter (MPS) scheme, but the Reagan Administration found this faulty and declared in December 1981 that '. . . initial deployment will be in Minuteman silos. At least 40 MXs will be deployed, with the first unit of 10 missiles operational in December 1986. The specific location will be determined in Spring 1982 . . . In addition, the Air Force has initiated R&D to find the best long-term option . . . The options include the following: ballistic missile defence of silo-based or deceptively-based missiles; deep basing scheme (DBS) in underground citadels; and air-mobile basing . . . Congress approved $1,900m for FY 1982 and some $2,500m has been spent to date. The cost to produce 226 missiles and deploy 40 in Minuteman silos is estimated at $1,800-1,900m in 1982 dollars . . .'

Next, the Armed Services Committee rejected Minuteman-silo basing and asked for a permanent basing plan by December 1, 1982. This resulted in yet further suggestions, notably DUB (deep underground basing) about 3,280ft (1,000m) down in rock with a self-contained tunnelling machine for each missile launch capsule and crew, and CSB (closely-spaced basing). The latter (also called 'dense pack') relied on the fratricide effect, where debris from the nuclear explosion of one, incoming warhead disables those following. President Reagan approved CSB in May 1982, for 100 missiles spaced 1,640ft (500m) apart over a region almost four miles (6km) across, but, in the event, 50 Peacekeepers are now being deployed in former Minuteman III silos at Warren Air Force Base in Wyoming. The first missile was installed in early 1986 and the tenth was operational by the end of the year, thus meeting the deadline set in December 1981. Better communications and control systems are being installed and more sophisticated shock absorber devices fitted, but the silos are not being further hardened, a plan to 'superharden' them to 5,000psi (365kg/cm^2) having been cancelled.

As of late 1984, Congress had authorised 50 operational Peacekeepers, although the Administration continued to request 100. Regardless of the final number deployed, the USAF has stated that it requires an additional 123 'test missiles' for use over the system's planned 15-year life-span. Planned usage of these missiles is eight flight tests per year for three years followed by seven per year for the following 12 years (total 108), plus one per year for ground testing and inspection (total 15).

Deployment: 1987 plans called for a deployment of 50 missiles only, to replace Minuteman IIIs and using the same silo sites. As of end 1987 14 had reached IOC at FE Warren AFB, Wy. The Reagan Administration anticipated obtaining authority for a further 50 Peacekeepers for which, according to then Secretary of Defense, Caspar Weinberger, 'several potential basing modes' were being studied, including at least one form of mobile basing.

In February 1987 it was announced that ten sites had been identified as potential 'rail garrisons', where Peacekeepers would be maintained in peacetime, deploying to classified locations in tension and war.

Employment: With a 0.05nm (100m) CEP and 335KT yield the Peacekeeper's W-87 warheads are almost certainly the most effective of any currently in use. It can, therefore, be assumed that they are capable of attacking successfully any hardened targets, including 'super-hardened' ICBM silos and 'leadership bunkers'.

SS-11

Status: In service
Dimensions: Length 62ft 4in (19m); diameter 96in (244cm)
Range: Mod 1 — 6,000nm (11,000km); Mod 2 — 7,000nm (13,000km);
Mod 3 — 5,710nm (10,600km)
Launch weight: 105,820lb (48,000kg)
Throw weight: Mod 1 — 2,200lb (998kg); Mods 2/3 — 2,500lb (1,134kg)
Propulsion: Two-stage; storable-liquid; hot launch
Guidance: Inertial
Warhead: Mod 1 — 1 x 1MT; Mod 2 — 1 x 1MT; Mod 3 — 3 x 250KT (MRV)
CEP: Mod 1 — 0.75nm (1,400m); Mods 2/3 — 0.59m (1,100m)

Development: SS-11 (Soviet designation not known) entered service in 1966 and has since served in three major variants. The missile is a little longer than the USAF's Minuteman, but much fatter and carries a much greater payload. At one time it was thought that SS-11 was launched using a cold-launch technique, but this has since been proved wrong. Two stages of the missile use storable liquid propellant, the first having four gimballed chambers. At the 1971 SALT I talks it was agreed that the SS-11 filled 970 silos, with 66 more being built.

The Mod 1 has a large single warhead, which at one time was reported to have a 20MT capability. Mod 2 was an upgraded Mod 1 with slightly greater range and throw-weight, penaids, and a more accurate warhead; CEP was 0.59nm (1,100m) compared to Mod 1's 0.75nm (1,400m). Mod 3 was the first Soviet ICBM with MRV, the first three warhead test being detected in 1969;

Left: Deployment of the successful SS-11 peaked at 1,036.

some 60 Mod 3s have been in service since 1973. Just over half the 970 SS-11s were replaced by SS-17 and SS-19 in the late 1970s, but some 450 still remain in service. However, more SS-11s are now being deactivated as the road-mobile SS-25 is deployed, on an apparent scale of 10 SS-11s for 9 SS-25s.

Deployment: Once deployed in greater numbers than any other missile system (numbers peaked at 1,036 in 1972), the number of SS-11s currently in service is 440, of which 20 are estimated to be Mod 1 and the remainder a mix of Mods 2 and 3. These 400 missiles are located in two main areas: Kozelsk, Teykovo and Perm in Western USSR, and at Gladkaya, Drovyanaya, Svobod-nyy and Olovyannaya in the Far East.

Employment: SS-11 Mod 1 and Mod 2 both have large, single warheads. They are not particularly accurate and are probably targeted against large, soft, area, 'counter-value' targets, such as cities, industrial complexes, and unprotected military installations.

The SS-11 Mod 3 has three MRV and was almost certainly designed to attack US ICBM silos; indeed, data obtained from Soviet tests show that the 'footprint' almost exactly matched the disposition of Minuteman silos, a technique pioneered by SS-9 Mod 4. However, there are now much more accurate and suitable warheads in the Soviet strategic arsenal and SS-11 Mod 3 may, if still targeted against the USA, have been switched to other targets.

The placing of the SS-11 fields in the Soviet Far East is noteworthy. They may well be intended to cover targets in China, Japan and other Asian countries. The SS-11 Mod 3 would still have a role here, targeted against the small number of Chinese missile sites.

It is probable that SS-11 Mods 1 and 2 are capable of fairly rapid retargeting on the ground. Retargeting SS-11 Mod 3 is, however, more likely to be a somewhat protracted affair.

Below: The November 1973 parade in Red Square, with two SS-11 Sego ICBMs in their transport containers.

SS-13

Status: In service
Dimensions: Length 65ft 7in (20m); diameter 67in (170cm)
Range: 5,000nm (9,400km)
Launch weight: 77,160lb (35,000kg)
Throw weight: 1,300lb (590kg)
Propulsion: Three-stage; solid-liquid; hot launch
Guidance: Inertial
Warhead: 1x600-750KT
CEP: 1.00nm (1,852m)

Development: This unusual missile (Soviet designation: RS-12) was the first Soviet ICBM to use solid fuel. Unlike any other known Soviet large missile, it comprises three stages, each with four TVC nozzles, linked together by open Warren-girder trusses, a configuration only matched by Chinese missiles, such as the CSS-3. SS-13 was developed in parallel with SS-11, but is somewhat smaller. It was shown publicly in May 1965 and entered service 1968.

Below: An SS-13 in an 'iron maiden' transport container, giving a good view of the second and third stages.

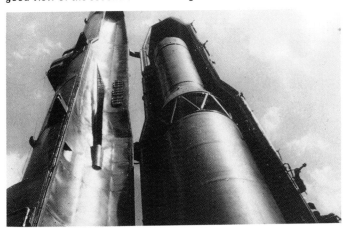

SS-17

Status: In service
Dimensions: Length 69ft (21m); diameter 82.8in (210cm)
Range: 5,400nm (10,000km)
Launch weight: 143,300lb (65,000kg)
Throw weight: 6,400lb (2,903kg)
Propulsion: Two-stage; storable liquid; cold launch
Guidance: Inertial
Warhead: Mod 1 — 4x200KT (MIRV); Mod 2 — 1x3.6MT; Mod 3 — 4x750KT (MIRV)
CEP: 0.22nm (400m)

Development: The SS-17 (Soviet designation: RS-16) was developed in parallel with (indeed, possibly in competition with) the SS-19 and is a successor to the SS-11, in many of whose former silos it is installed. Slightly larger

Total deployment is 60, all of them based around Yoshkar Ola, near the Plesetsk test centre; these have now been in service for 20 years. No MRV version has been developed, but it is thought that the two top stages were used to produce the SS-14, a land-mobile IRBM. Indeed, there were reports in the early 1970s that the SS-13 might be used in a mobile role, but, as far as is known, it has only ever been deployed in silos. The SS-25 missile is claimed by the USSR to be a modification of SS-13 as permitted in SALT II, but the USA disputes this. The USSR flew two SS-13 in 1986 to allow the USA to observe the missile in flight and thus compare it with their data on SS-25.

Quite what SS-13 contributes to the Soviet strategic arsenal has never become fully clear, but it must be presumed to serve a valuable purpose as the comparatively small production run must have been expensive and the maintenance of such a 'one-off' design a logistic headache for many years. It may be assumed that SS-13 will be phased out of service in the not too distant future.

Deployment: 60 missiles at Yoshkar Ola.
Employment: With a relatively poor CEP and a yield in the 600-750KT region, SS-13 could only be targeted against large, area, relatively soft targets in North America, Europe or Asia. Retargeting should be possible.

Below: Trailer-borne SS-13 ICBMs are paraded in Red Square. This missile has three stages, linked by girder trusses.

than the SS-11, the SS-17, uses liquid propellant, but utilises cold-launch techniques — the missile is expelled from its silo by a gas generator and first-stage ignition only takes place when well clear of the silo, thus not damaging the silo and enabling it to be re-used. The missile is placed in the silo in its launch canister, which further protects the silo during launch and also facilitates reloading.

SS-17 Mod 1 carries four MIRV warheads, each of not less than 200KT yield. SS-17 Mod 2 carries a single high yield RV. The principal service version, however, is the Mod 3.

Deployment: 150 in silos at Yedrovo and Kostroma in north western USSR.
Employment: SS-17 Mod 3 is clearly not considered by the US to be in the first league of Soviet ICBMs. US sources describe it as a: 'somewhat less capable ICBM than the SS-19, but [with] similar targeting flexibility.' It can, therefore, be assumed that, despite the size and relative accuracy of the MIRVs, the hard-target kill ability of the SS-17 is not great. It may well, therefore, be targeted upon military bases, airfields, and less well protected hard targets rather than on missile silos and command centres.

SS-18

Status: In service
Dimensions: Length 108ft 3in (33m); diameter 117.6in (300cm)
Range: Mod 1 — 6,480nm (12,000km); Mod 2/4 — 5,940nm (11,000km);
Mod 3 — 8,640nm (16,000km)
Launch weight: 171,985lb (78,000kg)
Throw weight: 16,700lb (7,575kg)
Propulsion: Two-stage; liquid fuel; cold launch
Guidance: Inertial
Warhead: Mod 1 — 1x25MT; Mod 2 — 8 or 10x500KT MIRV; Mod 3 —
1x20MT; Mod 4 — 10x550KT MIRV
CEP: 0.14nm (260m)

Development: The SS-18 (Soviet designation: RS-20) was developed in the late 1960s as the successor to the SS-9 and is by far the largest of the current (fourth) generation of Soviet ICBMs; in fact, with the retirement of the last US Titan II in 1987 the SS-18 is much the largest of the currently deployed ICBMs, and has by far the largest throw-weight. It was first deployed in 1974 in former SS-9 silos, which were modified and upgraded to take the new missile. These silos have been further upgraded in the early 1980s and are now reported to be able to withstand an overpressure of 5,000psi (365kg/cm²), designated by the USA (and deservedly so!) as 'superhardening'. Deployment continued until 1982, since when the numbers have remained unchanged at 308, with six launch complexes in a large semi-circle around the Tyuratam Missile test centre in Central USSR.

The first version, Mod 1, has a large single warhead, as has the Mod 3

SS-19

Status: In service
Dimensions: Length 78ft 8in (24m); diameter 92.64in (235cm)
Range: 5,400nm (10,000km)
Launch weight: 77,160lb (35,000kg)
Throw weight: 7,500lb (3,402kg)
Propulsion: Two-stage; liquid fuel; hot launch
Guidance: Inertial
Warhead: Mod 1 — 6x200KT MIRV; Mod 2 — 1x4MT; Mod 3 — 6x550KT
MIRV
CEP: 0.22nm (400m)

Development: Designed in parallel with the SS-17 as a replacement for the SS-11, the SS-19 (Soviet designation: RS-18) has undoubtedly proved the more successful of the two. 360 are deployed, making it currently the most numerous Soviet ICBM. Unlike the cold-launched SS-17 and SS-18, the SS-19 uses hot-launch techniques, although the provision of a launch canister restricts the amount of damage done to the silo. Indeed, if the US theory that SS-17 and SS-19 were developed in competition with each other is not correct, then it could be argued that SS-19 was a typical Russian insurance policy, using tried and tested techniques such as liquid fuel and hot launch, against the possible failure of the more radical SS-17.

All SS-19 sites lie in the western USSR and the predictions that this missile would replace SS-11s in the east have not transpired. SS-19 Mod 1 has four to six MIRVs of about 200KT each and the Mod 2 a single, large RV; the Mod 3 has six 550KT MIRVs. The SS-19 was stated for some years to have a CEP of 0.16nm (300m), but in 1985 this was reassessed upwards to 0.22nm (400m).
Deployment: All SS-19 deployed are assumed to be Mod 3. The 360 missiles

(20MT). Mod 2 has eight or ten 500KT MIRVs, while Mod 4 has ten 500KT MIRVs, and for SALT II purposes all operationally deployed missiles are assumed to be of this type. It is reported by the London-based International Institute for Strategic Studies (IISS) that an SS-18 Mod 5 may be under development: cold-launched, this is estimated to deliver up to ten 750KT MIRVs over a 5,400nm (10,000km) range.

There are also suggestions that the SS-18 is capable of carrying more than 10 MIRVs. In two tests in 1978 and 1979 the SS-18 'bus' deployed the 10 MIRVs it was carrying and then 'dipped' or altered course several more times. Then, in a 1983 test the SS-18 'bus', which on this occasion was not carrying any RVs, also dipped 14 times. This can be interpreted two ways: either the bus can carry 14 MIRVs, or it can carry 10 MIRVs and four penetration aids, decoys or chaff dispensers. Opinion remains divided, although official US documents continue to show the SS-18 payload as '10 plus MIRVs'.

Deployment: All deployed SS-18s are assumed to be Mod 4 with 10 MIRVs, although some reports suggest that a number may actually be Mod 2s with less than 10 warheads. The SS-18s are in 308 missile silos in six sites, which form a large arc in the central USSR, stretching from Kartaly in the west through Dombarovsky, Imeni Gastello, Zhanzig Tobe and Aleysk to Uzhur in the east.

Recent US statements claim that one of the roles of the SA-12 SAM system will be to provide an ABM defence at SS-18 launch sites, in association with the Krasnoyarsk radar.

Employment: Described by the US Department of Defense as 'highly accurate', SS-18 is designed to attack US ICBM silos and other hardened targets. According to the US 'the SS-18 Mod 4 force currently deployed has the capability to destroy 65 to 80 percent of US ICBM silos using two warheads against each. Even after this type of attack, more than 1,000 SS-18 warheads would be available for further strikes against targets in the US.'

are in silos in four sites in the western USSR at Kozelsk, Derazhnaya, Pervomaysk and Tatischevo. All these sites are west of Moscow and that at Derazhnaya is the farthest west of any Soviet ICBM field.

Employment: SS-19 Mod 3 is said by the USA to be 'less accurate than the SS-18, [but it] has significant capability against all but hardened silos. It could also be used against targets in Eurasia.' The same report states that SS-19 'is more capable than SS-17'. It is, therefore, fairly safe to assume that SS-19 is targeted against counter-force targets, such as reasonably hardened military installations, but not against ICBM silos themselves, which are the province of the SS-18.

Right: The SS-18, a third generation Soviet ICBM.

Far right: 360 SS-19s are deployed in various regions of the western USSR.

SS-24

Status: In service
Dimensions (est.): Length 69ft (21m); diameter 93in (235cm)
Range: 5,495nm (10,000km)
Launch weight: Unknown
Throw weight (est.): 8,000lb (3,629kg)
Propulsion: Three-stage; solid fuel; mobile launcher; cold launch
Guidance: Inertial
Warhead: 8-10x100KT (MIRV)
CEP: 0.11nm (200m)

Development: The SS-24 (Soviet designation: RS-23) was the first modern ICBM to be deployed in a rail-mobile mode, when it entered the Soviet inventory in 1987. In the late 1950s, the USA had considered basing Minuteman I (which was then in development) in five squadrons each of ten trains made up of three to five missile launchers with split roofs and some six to nine supporting vehicles.
Deployment: SS-24 is deployed in a three unit train, with one erector/launcher carriage and two further carriages for support activites and the crew. It is believed that the trains will be based upon the test centre at Plesetsk for the purposes of maintenance and general support, but obviously at least some of the trains will always be away travelling around the vast Soviet railway system.

SS-25

Status: In service
Dimensions (est.): Length 59ft (18m); diameter 71in (180cm)
Range: 5,670nm (10,500km)
Launch weight (est.): 77,160lb (35,000kg)
Throw weight: 1,600lb (726kg)
Propulsion: Three-stage; solid fuel; mobile launcher
Guidance: Inertial
Warhead: 1x550KT
CEP: 0.11nm (200m)

Development: The deployment of the SS-25 (Soviet designation: SS-12M) is the latest development in the USSR's operational ICBM force. SS-25 is a road-mobile missile of about the same size as the US Minuteman III. It carries only one 550KT warhead, which is delivered with a high degree of accuracy.

The first 18 SS-25s were deployed in early 1985 and the Soviets removed 20 of the elderly SS-11s to compensate and keep within the SALT limits. By the end of 1985 45 SS-25s had been deployed in five regiments of nine launchers each. A total of 70 SS-11s had been retired by this stage; 50 for the SS-25s already fielded and a further 20 in anticipation of two further SS-25 regiments. A total of 72 in anticipation of two further SS-25 regiments. A total of 72 SS-25s are now in service, but more will doubtless follow.

The SS-25 is deployed on a massive 14-wheel vehicle, which appears to be similar to that used for SS-20, but with a further set of wheels. The missile is mounted in a launch tube set along the top of the vehicle and hinged at the rear. The assembly is raised to the vertical by hydraulic jacks for firing. The bases for the SS-25 consist of garages with sliding roofs and a number of other buildings to house the mobile support equipment. Presumably the sliding roof enables the launcher-erector to be tested and could also be used for a live launch in the last resort.

No modifications of SS-25 have yet been announced, despite the length of time the system has been under development. It would, however, appear

The Soviets also intend to deploy 100 SS-24s in silos currently being used by SS-17. There will be about 600 SS-24s deployed by the mid-1990s.
Employment: SS-24 has up to ten 100KT MIRV warheads and with its CEP of 0.11nm (200m) will be capable of attacking all but the very hardest targets.

Below: Artist's impression of SS-24 on a rail-mobile launcher. It is anticipated that there will be 400 missiles thus deployed, with others in silos, and fears are that they could negate the recent US silo-hardening programmes.

possible that a MIRVed version is under development. It was during the flight testing of SS-25 that the Soviets first used encryption in their telemetry down-links, which the US claims to be in contravention of SALT II.
Deployment: 72 launchers are currently in service. Three bases have so far been identified, all in north-western USSR, at Yurya, Verkhnaya Salda (both currently also SS-20 bases) and Yoshkar Ola (currently the only base for the 60 SS-13s). Emergency deployment areas for the mobile launchers would be within 100 miles (160km) of these bases and operational deployment anything up to 4-500 miles (640-800km) away. Other deployments are expected.
Employment: Because it is launched from a road-mobile launcher the SS-25 system is inherently reloadable and difficult to knock out. Indeed, the US speculates that SS-25, like SS-24, has been designed for use in a protracted nuclear war, where it would be used as a reserve weapon, intended to ride out the first wave of US attacks on the USSR and then retaliate against targets which could be selected and set into the warhead at the time. As a single warhead weapon SS-25 will be quickly and easily retargetable. SS-25 is capable of attacking all but the very hardest targets, but these would, in all probability, have been taken out in a first strike anyway.

Below: The road-mobile SS-25 can be launched from shelters. A follow-up version could be developed as a MIRV.

SSBS S-3

Status: In service
Dimensions: Length 45ft 11in (14m); diameter 59in (150cm)
Range: 1,890nm (3,500km)
Launch weight: 56,879lb (25,800kg)
Throw weight: Unknown
Propulsion: Two-stage; solid fuel; hot launch
Guidance: Inertial
Warhead: One TN-61 1.2MT
CEP: 0.45nm (834m)

Development: Although technically an Intermediate Range Ballistic Missile (IRBM) the Sol-Sol Ballistique Strategique (SSBS) S-3 is, in European terms, a strategic system. The first French missile was the S-2 which entered service in 1971, and since then France has maintained a force of 18 SSBS in two groups of nine missiles each. The second generation S-3 missile began development in 1973. This has the same first stage as the S-2 but with the P-6 second stage developed for the MSBS (SLBM) and a completely new 1.2MT warhead, incorporating penetration aids. The whole missile is hardened against EMP.

The first flight of the S-3 was in 1976, and it was in service use by 1980, when the Plateau d'Albion site became operational. A second site followed in 1982.

Despite the vulnerability of these sites, plans for a third group of nine missiles were abandoned in 1974. A new system — 'SX' — is being examined, with a final decision due in 1988-90, although it now seems somewhat unlikely that France will incur the expense of developing a third generation IRBM/ICBM, even though the technological and industrial capacity clearly exists. It has been announced by the French Defence Ministry that the SSBN/SLBM force will be the primary strategic system in the future, but no date for the withdrawal of SSBS S-3 or the termination of SX has been announced.

Deployment: All 18 SSBS S-3 are located at the St Christol airbase on the Plateau d'Albion in Haute Provence. They are divided into two groups of nine missiles with individual silos some 3 miles (5km) apart. Reaction time is stated to be some 200 seconds.

Below: A single-warheaded SSBS SS-2 in its silo.

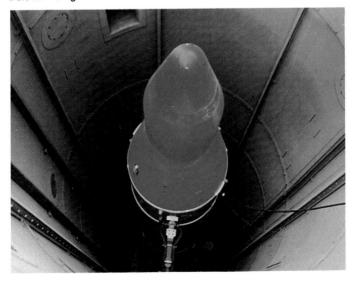

Employment: With its total of just 18 powerful, but relatively inaccurate, single warheads, the S-3 force is unlikely to be targeted against anything other than large, soft, counter-value targets, such as cities or industrial complexes. However, the S-3s must not be viewed in isolation, but in combination with the Mirage IV and SSBN/SLBM force, as part of a co-ordinated national force. The major problem facing the French would be when to launch the S-3s, since such a few silos in a relatively small area would be a fairly easy target for a fraction of the Soviet missile inventory and the only realistic escape from this would be to 'launch-on-warning'.

Below: France has a total of 18 SSBS S-3 missiles deployed in two sites. The S-3 is hardened against EMP.

CSS-4

Status: In service
Dimensions: Length 142ft 8in (43.5m); diameter 132in (335cm)
Range: 6,480nm (12,000km)
Launch weight: Unknown
Throw weight (est.): 3,086lb (1,400kg)
Propulsion: Three-stage; liquid fuel; hot launch
Guidance: Inertial
Warhead: 1x4-5MT
CEP: unknown

Development: The development of Chinese strategic weapons has been steady but not spectacular. Deployment so far indicates that the only perceived enemy is the USSR. A number of missile systems have been developed, designated, 'CSS − ' (Chinese, Surface-to-Surface) by the USA and 'Dong Feng − (East Wind) by the Chinese themselves.

To confuse the issue, the West did not apparently record the deployment of DF-1 and thus CSS-1 is DF-2, CSS-2 is DF-3, CSS-3 is DF-4 and CSS-4 is DF-5.

The CSS-1, a medium-range ballistic missile (MRBM) with a 20KT warhead entered service in 1966 and about 50 are still deployed in north-west China. CSS-1 has a range of approximately 550nm (1,019km) and is presumed to be aimed at targets in the eastern USSR.

CSS-2, a single-stage, 1,374nm (2,544km) range Intermediate Range Ballistic Missile (IRBM), has a 2-3MT warhead; it began deployment in the 1970s and between 85 and 125 are now in service. This missile is presumably targeted against large population centres in central and eastern USSR, but its

AS-15/SS-N-21/SS-C-4

Status: AS-15 in service; SS-N-21/SS-C-4 − under development
Dimensions: Length 22ft 7in (6.9m); body diameter 24in (60cm); wing span 11ft 4in (3.44m)
Performance: Cruise about Mach 0.7; range 1,620nm (3,000km)
Weight: At launch 2,825lb (1,282kg)
Propulsion: One small turbofan
Guidance: Inertial system
Warhead: One 250KT nuclear warhead

Development: Soviet bomber aircraft have long been fitted with long-range cruise missiles such as the AS-4, -5, -6, -7 and -8, to extend their range and to enable them to stand-off from strong defences. However, following the lead given by the USA, the Soviet armed forces have now joined together to develop a common cruise missile. The air-launch version (AS-15) is already in service, while versions for launching from a submarine (SS-N-21) and from a ground launcher (SS-C-4) are under development. (The sea-based version will be launched from a standard 21in (53cm) torpedo tube.)

An even newer cruise missile − SS-NX-24 − is reported to be under development. This very large, swept-wing cruise-missile may well have an intercontinental range. The Soviets appear to intend to deploy land- and submarine-launched versions, but it is so large that it appears unlikely that an air-launched version is contemplated.

Deployment: AS-15 became operational in 1984 on the specially built Bear-H ALCM carrier aircraft. It is also expected to arm the Blackjack when that aircraft comes into service.

Employment: AS-15's range is considerably greater than that of the US ALCM and gives the carrier aircraft the opportunity to stand-off from much

range is also sufficient to threaten Japan and India.

The next Chinese ballistic missile system — the CSS-3 — has a range of 4,120nm (7,630km), which places it roughly between an IRBM and an ICBM. It is a two-stage, liquid-fuelled missile with a 1-3MT warhead. It was the first Chinese ballistic missile to be launched from silos (CSS-1 and -2 are road-mobile) and has been deployed at a very slow rate; it now seems that no more than the current 10 are planned. Indeed, it may well be that it was simply a precursor on the way to the true ICBM — the CSS-4.

Deployment: Like CSS-3, production and deployment of CSS-4 has been very limited, and only about ten are believed to be in service. This could be for one of several reasons. It may be that China does not want to antagonise either the USSR or the USA by deploying a large force of ICBMs. Alternatively, China may have decided to concentrate its long-term efforts on an SSBB/SLBM force, in which case, the CSS-3 and -4 would have been developed as a safeguard against the failure of the much more ambitious and technically risky naval programme. In any case, CSS-4 is deployed in silos at an unknown site within western China.

Employment: CSS-4's range, reliably estimated to be in excess of 6,000nm (11,112km), enables it to strike any target in the USSR, Europe or the USA, thus giving the Chinese (should they require it) what the French once referred to as a 'touts azimuth' capability. Its primary significance lies in its ability to strike at targets in European USSR; the first time that the Chinese have been able to do so. Ten single warheads, possibly without sophisticated penaids for the next few years, may not be able to guarantee penetration of Moscow's strategic defences, although the development of CSS-4 is said to have had a strong influence on the Soviet development of the new Moscow ABM system. CSS-4 could, however, certainly succeed against at least four or five other major urban-industrial complexes in the Soviet heartland.

greater distances. One of its intended roles would undoubtedly be for attacks on the North American mainland.

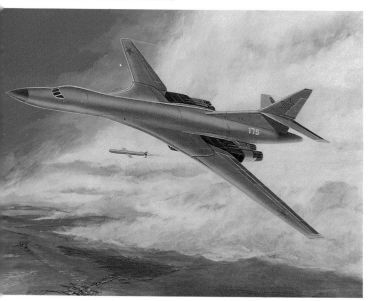

Above: The nuclear-armed AS-15 cruise missile will shortly be deployed on the Blackjack bomber (depicted here).

Air-Launched Cruise Missile (ALCM)

Status: In service
Dimensions: Length 20ft 8in (6.32m); body diameter 27.3in (693mm); wing span 12ft (3.66m)
Performance: Cruise about Mach 0.65; terminal speed Mach 0.8; range 1,350nm (2,500km)
Weight: At launch 2,825lb (1,282kg)
Propulsion: One Williams F107-101 turbofan with sea-level rating of 600lb (272kg) static thrust
Guidance: SAGEM E65 inertial system
Warhead: W-80 nuclear weapon

Development: The original ALCM was interchangeable with SRAM so that B-52G or -H could carry eight on the internal launcher plus 12 externally. This influenced the fuselage shape, which is essentially triangular, and necessitated retractable wings, tail and engine-air duct. In 1976 the decision was made to make the system as close as possible to the AGM-109 Tomahawk, but the guidance packages are not identical.

The AGM-86A ALCM first flew at White Sands Missile Range on March 5, 1976 and the first five flights were not very successful. Things improved after that, but nevertheless in 1980 it was decided to develop a 30 per cent longer

ASMP

Status: In service
Dimensions: Length 17ft 8in (5.38m); body diameter 15in (38cm); width across inlet ducts about 32.2in (82cm); wing span 3ft 2in (0.96m)
Performance: Speed about Mach 4; range at high altitude 135nm (250km) at Mach 3; range at low altitude 43nm (80km) at Mach 2
Weight: At launch 1,852lb (840kg)
Propulsion: Integrated rocket/ram-jet, using SNPE rocket with Statolite smokeless filling and Aérospatiale advanced kerosene-fuelled ramjet
Guidance: SAGEM E65 inertial system
Warhead: One 300KT nuclear warhead

Development: The Air/Sol Moyenne Portée (ASMP) is giving a new lease of life to the Mirage IV strategic bomber force. ASMP was initiated in 1971 and after a somewhat protracted development is now in service, 18 bombers being converted to Mirage IVP to take the missile.

Propulsion is by a liquid-fuelled (kerosene) ramjet with an integral booster. The latter accelerates the missile to Mach 2 in some five seconds at which point the missile's tail-cone and air inlet blanks are jettisoned and kerosene is pressure-fed into the ramjet sustainer motor.

ASMP is programmed prior to take-off with speed, altitude and navigation requirements and final target data is fed in via a cassette while the missile is on its launch pylon. Airborne, but before release, the inertial guidance system is aligned with that of the aircraft and the digital computer is given any last minute changes of flight-plan. The missile is launched at speeds of between Mach 0.6 and 0.9. ASMP can follow either high- or low-level flight profiles, but in the latter case does not have an 'intelligent' terrain-following capability, although the flight-path can be programmed to take advantage of terrain-masking.
Deployment: Eighteen operational missiles have been allocated to the 18 Mirage IVPs in the strategic role; there are also test and training missiles.

version with increased fuel, under the designation AGM-86B. This version has double the range for the same payload and tests were very successful. As a result an order was placed in 1980 for 3,418 missiles, later increased to 3,780.

Two new missiles are being developed: the Advanced Cruise Missile (ACM) and SRAM II. Both will be more capable than their predecessors, and the ACM will also incorporate 'stealth' technology.

Deployment: ALCM is deployed on B-52G, B-52H and B-1.

Below: Air-Launched Cruise Missiles (ALCM) on a B-52 bomber.

Employment: The Mirage IVA strategic bombers, refuelled by C-135F tankers and armed with AN-11 or AN-22 free-fall nuclear weapons, had a key role in France's *force de dissuasion*. However, their difficulties in reaching and then returning from targets deep in the Soviet Union was becoming problematical. The ASMP, although it does not have a particularly great range, gives the bomber force a further lease of life and continued effectiveness through to the mid-1990s, at least.

Below: The ASMP missile, seen here with a Mirage 2000 aircraft, although initial and planned deployment is with converted Mirage IVP bombers. Although range has been greatly increased from initial specifications, there are doubts as to whether the associated Antilope 5 radar can acquire targets at 135nm (250km). After the ASMP's boost to supersonic speed, twin side inlets provide air for the ramjet.

SRAM (AGM-69)

Status: In service
Dimensions: Length 14ft (4.27m); body diameter 17.5in (44.5cm)
Performance: Speed Mach 2.8-3.2; range variable depending upon flight profile, between 30 and 91nm (56 to 169km)
Weight: At launch 2,230lb (1,012kg)
Propulsion: LPC-415 solid propellant, two-pulse rocket motor
Guidance: Inertial system
Warhead: One 200KT W-69 weapon

Development: Studies for a Short-Range Attack Missile (SRAM) began in 1963, leading to first flight in 1969 and IOC in early 1972. A total of 1,500 AGM-69As were produced.

SRAM is fitted with Singer-Kearfott inertial guidance and a Delco computer. This guidance package enables it to follow four very different flight profiles: semi-ballistic; terrain-following; pull-up from 'under-the-radar' followed by inertial dive; and combined inertial and terrain following.

Deployment: Of 1,500 missiles manufactured some 1,140 remain operational, 1,020 of them with the B-52 force. B-52s can carry up to 20 SRAM: eight on a rotary launcher in the bomb-bay, plus six in two groups of three on underwing pylons. (The FB-111 tactical bomber can carry up to six SRAM.)

Employment: SRAM can be launched from high or low altitude, and can be retargeted from the aircraft prior to launch. It is likely to be used against heavily defended targets such as air defence missile sites, radar installations, airfields, or other military targets.

Below: The Boeing AGM-69 Short-Range Attack Missile (SRAM) carries a 200KT W-69 nuclear warhead. Range depends upon launch height and mission profile.

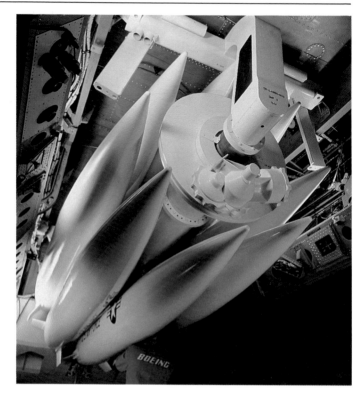

Above: Eight rounds loaded on the revolving launcher installed in the aft bomb bay of a SAC B-52G.

Below: USAF FB-111As can carry two SRAM on swivelling pylons under each wing, plus two in the internal bomb bay.

Delta I/II/III/IV

Status: In service
Built: Delta I — 1973 to 1977; Delta II — 1973 to 1975; Delta III — 1976 to 1981; Delta IV — 1984 onwards
Displacement: Delta I — 10,000 tons submerged; Delta II — 11,400 tons submerged; Delta III — 13,250 tons submerged; Delta IV — 14,250 tons submerged
Dimensions: Delta I — length 459ft (140m); Delta II/III — length 508ft 6in (152.7m); Delta IV — length 538ft (164m); Delta I/II/III/IV — beam 39ft 5in (11.6m); Delta I/II/III/IV — draught 28ft 5in (10m)
Performance: Pressurized-water nuclear reactors; 60,000shp; two shafts; 25 knots dived; normal operating depth 1,180ft (360m)
Operating Pattern: Sea endurance 90 days
Weapons: SLBM: Delta I — 12 SS-N-8; Delta II — 16 SS-N-8; Delta III — 16 SS-N-18; Delta IV — 16 SS-N-23. Torpedo Tubes: Six 21in (53cm) tubes with twelve reloads
Complement: Delta I — 120; Delta II/III/IV — 132

Development: Before 1973, the US Navy had major advantages in the quality and performance of its SLBMs, but in that year the Soviet Navy introduced its SS-N-8 missile with a range of more than 4,170nm (7,720km) and a Circular Error Probable (CEP) of only 0.84nm (1,550m). This weapon outranged the Poseidon, at that time the latest US SLBM, although the Soviet missile, unlike its American counterpart, was not MIRVed and still retained the more volatile liquid fuel of earlier Soviet SLBMs. Initial trials of the SS-N-8 were carried out in a converted Hotel III SSBN.

SS-N-8 first went to sea as an operational system in the new Delta I SSBN, which had been designed around it, although using the basic design of the earlier Yankee Class as the starting point. The Delta I carries only 12 missiles in two rows of six abaft the sail. These boats were built at Komsomolsk on the Pacific coast and at Severodvinsk in the Artic, where a second slipway was constructed to expedite the production of these large and impressive boats. The four Delta IIs, which were lengthened versions of the Delta I carrying 16 missiles, were also built at Severodvinsk. This enabled them to match the con-

temporary Western SSBNs, all of which had 16 missiles.

The Delta III is somewhat longer than its predecessors and carries 16 of the even more advanced SS-N-18 missiles, of which the latest Mod 3 has a range of some 3,448nm (3,510km) and mounts MIRVed warheads. Due to the greater length of the SS-N-18 missile the superstructure of the Delta III abaft the sail is even higher than on the Delta I and II and the hydrodynamic matching of the two is very poor. This makes them very noisy, and they would be easy to detect and identify anywhere near a NATO ASW force.

Surprisingly, despite the commissioning of the first elements of the more advanced Typhoon class in 1983, yet another new version of the Delta class — Delta IV — appeared in 1984. This carries 16 of another new missile, the SS-N-23, a liquid-fuelled replacement for the SS-N-18, with a range of 4,480nm (8,300km) and carrying up to 10 MIRVs. A fairing on the whaleback casing and a bracket further aft suggest that a towed array is used. The fin has also been modified and is now similar in height and outline to that fitted on the Oscar class SSGN.

It would seem that the Delta class is destined to remain in production for some time, although a replacement is almost certainly on the drawing-boards. The SS-N-23 SLBM will be retrofitted to Delta III submarines, but it is too large for the Delta Is and IIs.

Class Notes: Delta I — 18 in service; Delta II — four in service; Delta III — 14 in service; Delta IV — three in service, more building.

Deployment: Of the 39 Delta class SSBNs in service, 23 are based with the Northern Fleet: nine Delta Is, all four Delta IIs, seven Delta IIIs and all three of the currently-building Delta IV. The remaining 16 are with the Pacific Fleet: nine Delta Is and seven Delta IIIs. However, as is normal Soviet Navy practice, only a small proportion of these are on patrol at any one time.

The 1985 edition of *'Soviet Military Power'* (published annually by the US Department of Defense) shows a Delta IV surfaced among ice firing its missiles, clearly indicating Arctic deployment capabilities. Delta I, II and III, however, may not have the same capability, although they pose a significant threat to the United States, because they can hit North America from launching areas in the Sea of Okhotsk and the Barents Sea — the so-called 'SSBN sanctuaries'.

Below: The Delta I SSBN carries 12 SS-N-8 SLBMs.

Lafayette/Franklin (SSBN-616)

Built: 1961-1966
Displacement: 7,250 tons surfaced; 8,250 tons submerged
Dimensions: Length overall 425ft (129.5m); beam 33ft (10.1m); draught 31.5ft (10.1m)
Performance: One pressurized-water cooled SW5 nuclear reactor; two geared turbines, 15,000shp; 1 shaft; 30-plus knots dived; operating depth greater than 984ft (300m)
Operating Pattern: Sixty-eight day patrol; 32 day short refit; 16 months long refit every six years (three boats on nine-year cycle). Force availability 55 per cent.
Weapons: Missiles — Sixteen tubes for Poseidon C-3 (18 boats); sixteen tubes for Trident I (C-4) (12 boats); Torpedo tubes — Four 21in (53cm).
Complement: 147

Development: The 30 Lafayette/Franklin class boats were the definitive US SSBNs of the 1960s and 1970s. The initial Lafayettes were slightly enlarged and improved versions of the Ethan Allen design and are almost indistinguishable (at least externally) from that class. The last 12 of the class, however, differ considerably from the earlier boats and are officially referred to as the Benjamin Franklin class. They have improved, quieter machinery and 28 more crew.

The first eight Lafayettes were originally fitted with Polaris A-2 missiles, while all the remaining boats had the improved Polaris A-3, with a range of 2,855 miles (4,594km) and three 200KT MRV warheads. A further difference is that the first five boats launched their missiles with compressed air, but the remainder use a rocket motor to produce a gas-steam mixture to eject the missiles from their tubes. All Lafayettes were converted to take the Poseidon C-3 SLBM between 1970 and 1977. Then, in a further conversion programme, twelve of these Poseidon boats were refitted between 1978 to 1985 to take the larger, three-stage, Trident I C-4 missile; USS *Francis Scott Key* (SSBN-657) started the first Trident I (C-4) missile patrol on October 10, 1979.

Although these SSBNs do not have the underwater performance of the SSNs they have a respectable capability against surface ships and other submarines and are armed with conventional or wire-guided torpedoes and Subroc. Normally, however, they would attempt to evade detection or contact.

Class Notes: Thirty boats were built (18 Lafayette class; 12 Franklin class). Three of the class have been deactivated to comply with SALT II provisions as Ohio boats are commissioned and more will follow. To summarise a complicated class, the position as at December 31, 1987 was that there were 27 boats in service: 15 armed with Poseidon (C-3) (9 Lafayette, 6 Franklin) and 12 armed with Trident I (C-4) (6 Lafayette, 6 Franklin).

Deployment: All boats of both classes belong to the Atlantic Fleet and the Trident I (C-4) boats are home-ported at King's Bay, Georgia. The Poseidon boats patrol further out into open ocean than do those vessels armed with Trident.

Below: The USS Lafayette (SSBN-616), name-ship of a very successful class. Seventeen other subs were built in the same class — three have been deactivated.

Le Redoutable

Status: In service
Built: 1967-1985
Displacement: 8,045 tons surfaced; 8,940 tons submerged
Dimensions: Length overall 422.5ft (128.7m); beam 34.9ft (10.6m); draught 32.9ft (10m)
Performance: One pressurized, water-cooled nuclear reactor; geared steam turbines; two turbo-alternators; one electric motor; 16,000shp; one shaft; 20 knots surfaced, 25 knots dived
Operating Pattern: Assumed to be similar to US Navy Lafayette class SSBN, but with two always on patrol
Weapons: Missiles — Sixteen MSBS M-20 (first five boats); sixteen M-4/TN-70 (L'Inflexible on building and all except Le Foudroyant during refit; Torpedo tubes — Four 21in (53cm) for L5 and L7 torpedoes, and (in due course) SM39 missiles. Total 18
Complement: 135

Development: As with the British across the Channel, the French decided that it was necessary to build nuclear-powered ballistic missile submarines to ensure a viable national nuclear deterrent. Unlike the British, however, with their Polaris and Trident submarines, the French *force d'dissuasion* has been developed virtually independently of the USA, although some covert assistance may have been given. This has resulted in a much greater effort spread over a much longer timescale, and, at least in the earlier days, in heavier missiles carrying smaller warheads over a shorter range.

The Le Redoutable-class SSBNs were built to the same design philosophy as the American SSBNs in that they have two rows of eight missiles abaft the sail. However, unlike the Americans and the British, the French did not already have SSN designs which could be lengthened to accommodate the missile section.

The French SSBNs have pressurized water-cooled nuclear reactors and turbo-electric propulsion. They also have two auxiliary diesels that can be cut-in to provide power should the primary system fail; sufficient fuel is carried for 4,344 miles (8,045km). The forward hydroplanes are mounted on the fin as in US Navy SSBNs.

French policy is to have three SSBN hulls available at any one time, of which two must be on patrol. To achieve this the sixth boat, L'Inflexible, was ordered in 1979 and entered service in 1985. This is of an interim design, essentially an improved Le Redoutable, incorporating a number of modifications based on experience with the earlier boats and on recent technological developments. L'Inflexible, for example, can dive some 328ft (100m) deeper than her predecessors.

The first four boats were all modified to take the Mer-Sol Ballistique Stratégique (MSBS) M-2, but have subsequently been modified again to take the M-20. The fifth boat was constructed from the outset to take the latter missile. An even better missile — the M-4 — with a MIRVed warhead entered service in 1985 on L'Inflexible. This has a range in excess of 2,160nm (4,000km) and is armed with six of the new 150KT warheads. Le Tonnant will be modified for the M-4 during her next long refit, as will all other of the earlier boats with the exception of the first, Le Redoutable, which is considered too old. All boats are also armed with four 21in (53cm) bow-mounted torpedo tubes; 18 torpedoes being carried.

The French SSBN/SLBM programme is a major national achievement, although it is one that has been achieved at great (although obviously bearable) price. On November 13, 1981, President Mitterand visited Le Tonnant on patrol, following which he announced an order for a seventh SSBN, also of the interim class, for delivery in the mid-1980s, a clear endorsement of France's independent nuclear deterrent policy. It is planned to replace all five first-

generation boats with a totally new class in 1990-2000, beginning with *Le Redoutable* in 1995, the interim design boats being replaced later.

Class Notes: Six boats are in commission: five of the initial Le Redoutable class and one of the interim L'Inflexible class. The seventh SSBN is to be laid down in 1988 for commissioning in 1994.

Deployment: French policy is to have three SSBN hulls available at any one time, of which two must be on patrol. There have been tactical problems as a result of the short range of the earlier types of missile. The MSBS M-1 SLBM, for example, which was fitted in the first two boats, had a range of only 1,296nm (2,400km), but this has been progressively increased in successive missile systems. However, this short range meant that much longer transit times were necessary to reach the patrol areas and led to the requirement for more submarines than for the Royal Navy. All French SSBNs are home ported at Brest.

Below: Le Redoutable, the result of French determination.

Ohio (SSBN-726)

Status: In service
Built: 1976-1995
Displacement: 16,764 tons surfaced; 18,750 tons submerged
Dimensions: Length overall 560ft (170.7m); beam 42ft (12.8m); draught 36.5ft (11.13m)
Performance: One natural circulation, pressurized-water cooled S8G nuclear reactor; two geared turbines, 60,000shp; 1 shaft; 30-plus knots dived; operating depth 984ft (300m)
Operating Pattern: Seventy day patrol; 25 day short refit; 12 month long refit every nine years. Force availability 66 percent
Weapons: Missiles — Twenty four tubes for Trident I or II SLBM; Torpedo tubes — Four 21in (53cm)
Complement: 133

Development: While the programme of upgrading the later Polaris SLBM submarines to carry Poseidon was under way in the early 1970s the development of an entirely new missile was started. This missile, the Trident I (C-4) has a range of 3,837nm (7,100km), and is now in service aboard twelve converted Lafayette-class SSBNs. However, it was decided that, to take full advantage of these new missiles (and to accept the already-planned and slightly larger successor — the Trident II) a new class of larger SSBNs should be built. It was also decided to design the new boats to take 24 missiles rather than 16, a weapon load increase of 50 per cent. In addition, all the latest techniques, especially of quietening, were to be built-in.

Congress baulked initially at the enormous cost of the new system, but when the Soviet Navy introduced its own long-range SLBM, the 4,137nm (7,800km) SS-N-8 in the Delta class, US reaction was to authorize and speed-up the Trident programme. The first of the Ohio-class boats was laid down on April 10, 1976. The first eight of these purpose-built Trident submarines had joined the fleet by 1987 and twelve more were authorized.

The eventual number of Trident-carrying submarines depends upon two principal factors. The first is the outcome of the Strategic Arms Reduction-Talks (START) and the other is expense. Current US Navy plans are for a force of 24 Ohio, of which ten would be allocated to the Pacific Fleet and 14 to the Atlantic Fleet. With an anticipated availability of 66 percent, that would give an average of fifteen submarines at sea at anyone time, carrying a total of 360 missiles.

The Ohio-class SSBNs have 24 vertically-mounted missile launch tubes abaft the sail. The first eight boats have Trident I SLBMs, but will change to Trident II from the ninth boat on. Ohio-class SSBNs also have four bow-mounted torpedo tubes, firing conventional torpedoes.

Sensors include the BQQ-5 sonar system in the bows and a passive tactical towed sonar array, for which the cable and winch are mounted in the ballast tanks. The array itself is housed in a prominent fairing which runs along almost the entire length of the hull.

The first eight Ohio-class SSBNs are armed with 24 Trident I C-4 missiles, mounted vertically abaft the sail. The Trident II D-5 missile will be retrofitted into the first eight over the period 1991 to 1999. Trident II D-5, carries larger payloads and is more accurate than Trident I, thus providing the SSBN force with the potential to put 'hard' targets at risk — a significant expansion of the SSBN/SLBM role, which up to now has been as a survivable, second-strike, counter-value, deterrent system.

There is current debate in the US about the position from the late 1990s onwards when the last of the modified Lafayettes will be retired. As always there is pressure to find a less expensive alternative — not surprising in view of the cost: $1.8 billion per submarine in the 1985 budget. A further factor must be the possibility of a breakthrough in submarine detection (for example, from space-

based sensors) which might deprive SSBNs of their current relative immunity.
Class Notes: Current US plans are to build a total of 24 Ohio class SSBNs; of these eight are now in service; six are building; and five are ordered.
Deployment: Ohio class SSBNs will be home-ported at Bangor, Wash, on the west coast or Kings Bay, Georgia on the east coast of the USA, patrolling in the Pacific and Atlantic respectively. In both cases, the vessels are almost certain to undertake under-ice deployments, although there has never been any public acknowledgement of a US capability to surface among the ice and fire missiles.

Above: USS Ohio (SSBN-726), the US Navy's first purpose-built Trident submarine, before her launch ceremony.

Below: The USS Ohio. Her 24 Trident SLBMs are housed abaft her sail, as with all SSBNs bar the Soviet Typhoon class.

Resolution

Status: In service
Built: 1966-1969
Displacement: 7,600 tons surfaced; 8,500 tons submerged
Dimensions: Length overall 425ft (129.5m); beam 33ft (10.1m); draught 30ft (9.1m)
Performance: One pressurized, water-cooled nuclear reactor; geared steam turbines; 15,000shp; 1 shaft; 20 knots surfaced, 25 knots dived
Operating Pattern: Similar to USS Lafayette SSBN (qv). A minimum of one is always at sea but periodically there are two
Weapons: Missiles — Sixteen Polaris A-3/TK SLBM; Torpedo tubes — Six 21in (53cm)
Complement: 143

Development: In the late 1950s the British Government planned that the Royal Air Force would continue to provide the national strategic nuclear deterrent through the 1960s and the 1970s, using V-bombers armed with the US Skybolt missile. However, following the unilateral (and very unexpected) US decision to abandon Skybolt, President Kennedy agreed at the hastily-convened 1962 Nassau conference to provide Polaris A-3 missiles for installation on British-built SSBNs. An important feature of the agreement was that the British would provide the nuclear warheads and re-entry vehicles, thus enabling them to retain control over the use and targeting of the missiles.

Four submarines were built of a planned total of five, the last being cancelled in the Labour Government's 1965 Defence Review. The Resolution-class is

Below: HMS Resolution, the Royal Navy's first nuclear-powered ballistic missile submarine.

Right: Four SSBNs of the Resolution class were built, the fifth being cancelled in 1965.

generally similar to the US Lafayette-class SSBNs, although the Resolution's actual design was developed from that of the British Valiant-class SSNs, but with a missile compartment between the control centre and the reactor room. There are 16 vertically-mounted missile launch tubes abaft the sail, containing Polaris missiles. The first boat was commissioned on October 2, 1967, and the fourth and last on December 4, 1969.

Following prolonged debate, which has included detailed consideration of a variety of alternative options, the British Government announced its intention to purchase Trident II D-5 missiles from the USA. As with Polaris, an entirely British front-end will be fitted, to ensure national control of the system. Apart from replacing the elderly Polaris missiles the Royal Navy also needs to replace the Resolution-class SSBNs. which, although very reliable and successful, will be out-of-date by the beginning of the 1990s. Thus, the new missiles will be deployed in the new Vanguard class of British-designed and built SSBN. Four are currently planned, but, as with the Resolution class, the decision on the fifth will be taken later (in view of the escalating costs of the programme, this almost inevitably means that history will be repeated and the fifth boat will not be built). Construction of the new SSBNs started in 1987. They are expected in service in the early 1990s, with a life expectancy through to the 2020s at least.

Class Notes: Four in service.

Deployment: Because of the need always to have at least one boat in refit, the Royal Navy can only *guarantee* to have one boat on patrol at any one time, with a second just some of the time; average is 1.44. This has severe implications, as a nuclear deterrent may be based upon one single vessel. Many problems would have been avoided had the fifth boat been built, and it is noteworthy that the French, in a similar position to the British, decided from the start to have five boats, and have since gone on to build a sixth.

Typhoon

Status: In service
Built: 1978 onward
Displacement: 29,000 tons submerged
Dimensions: Length 561ft (171m); beam 75.45ft (23m); draught unknown
Performance: Two nuclear reactors, two steam turbines; 80,000shp; 2 shafts; 24 knots dived (see Background below)
Operating Pattern: Unknown
Weapons: SLBM — SS-N-20; Torpedo tubes — Six 21in (53cm), with conventional torpedoes, and possibly SS-N-15, SS-N-16 or SS-N-21
Complement: 150

Development: Persistent rumours in Western military circles were confirmed in November 1980 by the NATO announcement that the USSR had launched the first of the Typhoon-class SSBNs. This event created much interest, because, as the Delta-class had been a progressive development of the

Yankee-class, the Typhoon was, in fact, the first completely new Soviet SSBN design for some twenty years. But, even more than this, the interest centred on the sheer size of this enormous craft which has a submerged displacement of 29,000 tons and an overall length of 561ft (171m), making it by far the largest submarine ever built. Among many unusual features of the design is the 75.45ft (23m) beam. The normal length:beam ratio in the SSBNs is in the region of 13:1, but the extraordinary-girth of the Typhoon reduces this to 7:1. This may indicate a considerable degree of separation (up to 14-15ft — 4.3-4.6m) between concentric outer and inner hulls, or simply a huge inner hull. Most authorities agree, however, that the most probable explanation is that there are two separate side-by-side pressure hulls, surrounded by a single outer hull.

Another significant departure from previous practice is that the 20 missile ▶

Below: The Soviet Typhoon class SSBN. This picture does not give a true indication of the enormous size of this submarine, which is 478ft (170m) long, with a beam of 81ft (26m). It is thought to have two pressure hulls side-by-side within the streamlined outer casing.

▶ tubes are forward of the fin. The reason for this is not yet clear, although one possibility is that the propulsion machinery for such a huge vessel is so large and heavy that the missile compartment must be moved forward to compensate. It has been suggested that this might somehow be associated with the Typhoon's under-ice capability, although the Delta IV is also known to operate under the ice-cap, and seems to do so with the conventional layout with the missiles abaft the fin.

The principal armament of the Typhoon lies in its 20 SS-N-20 SLBMs located in launch canisters forward of the fin in two rows of ten. The SS-N-20 has between six and nine MIRVed warheads and a range of 4,482nm (8,300km). A battery of torpedo tubes is located forward of the missile compartment, and, apart from conventional torpedoes, this may well be used for cruise missiles (such as the SS-N-X-21) and minelaying; both weapons would be very useful if the Typhoon's role were to be in distant waters.

The speed of the Typhoon is a question that arouses much debate in the West. Conventional wisdom suggests twin nuclear reactors, twin screw and an underwater speed of about 25 to 30 knots. However, it is possible that the well-documented Soviet experiments in boundary-layer control may have reached fruition, in which case, and if allied to very powerful engines, a much higher speed could be feasible.

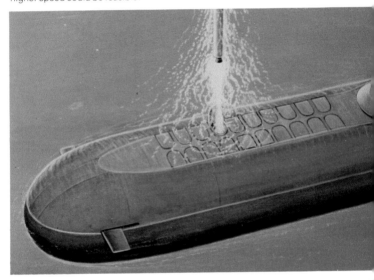

Xia

Status: In service
Built: 1978 onward
Displacement: 8,000 tons submerged
Dimensions: Length 321ft 6in (98m); beam 32ft 10in (10m); draught unknown
Performance: One pressurized, water-cooled nuclear reactor; turbo-electric drive; two shafts; 22 knots
Operating Pattern: A firm pattern will not be established until at least four boats are completed, but will then probably be similar to the USS Lafayette
Weapons: SLBM — 12 CSS-N-3; Torpedo tubes — Four (possibly six) 21in (53cm) with conventional torpedoes
Complement: 95

Class Notes: Four in service; one fitting out; four building. All eight will be in service by 1990.

Deployment: If it was to venture out into the open oceans this submarine would seem to be relatively easy for opposing ASW forces to detect — its very size facilitates detection by some means. Conversely, the large volume of the hull makes quietening, a major problem in SSBN design, rather easier. One possibility would seem to be that the Typhoon is simply intended to be a relatively invulnerable missile launching platform, required only to move out a short distance across the Barents Sea to the Arctic ice-cap and to loiter there, its time on station limited only by the endurance of the crew. For the latter, conditions can be assumed to be more spacious and comfortable than in any previous SSBN. There is, however, one other possibility: that the Typhoon is designed to operate for protracted periods a long way from its bases. The 4,482 mile (8,300km) range of its SS-N-20 SLBMs would certainly enable the Typhoon to operate in the southern oceans, thus posing a threat to the USA from a completely new direction, and causing an expensive realignment of its warning and detection radar systems. In fact, this submarine could be deployed anywhere in the world.

Below: SLBMs mounted before the sail make the Typhoon unique.

Development: Given its hostility towards the USA and then towards the Soviet Union, and its well-established submarine and missile industries, it was inevitable that the People's Republic of China should develop an SSBN/SLBM capability of its own. This has now reached fruition in the shape of the Xia class SSBN, armed with 12 CSS-N-3 SLBMs.

The Xia class (Xia is a Western nickname as the Chinese designation is not yet known) is being built at the Huludao yard, which is located some 124 miles (200km) northeast of Beijing, where the Han class SSNs are also built.

Class Notes: Two in service; two building; at least two more planned.

Deployment: Clearly the Chinese have a great deal of work to do in establishing operational patterns and in training men for an SSBN fleet; thus, sustained operational deployments cannot be expected for some years. The Xias can be expected to deploy in Pacific waters, their missiles targeted on the eastern USSR. Later deployments in the Indian Ocean will probably also be undertaken.

Yankee I/II

Status: In service
Built: Yankee I — 1966-71; Yankee II — 1975
Displacement: 9,600 tons submerged
Dimensions: Length 426ft 6in (130m); beam 39ft 5in (12m); draught 28ft 11in (8.8m)
Performance: Two nuclear reactors, steam turbines; 45,000shp; 2 shafts; 27 knots dived; operating depth 1,180ft (360m)
Operating Pattern: Sea endurance 90 days
Weapons: SLBM — (Yankee I) 16 SS-N-6; (Yankee II) 12 SS-N-17; Torpedo tubes — Six 21in (53cm) with conventional torpedoes
Complement: 120

Development: The Yankee class were the first Soviet purpose-built nuclear ballistic missile submarines to enter service, and (a decade after the Americans) they were the first Soviet SSBNs to mount SLBMs within the hull, as opposed to in the fin. The 16 missiles are arranged in two vertical rows of eight abaft the fin in a similar fashion to the US Polaris boats. The first 20 vessels were armed with the SS-N-6 Mod 1 (Sawfly) SLBM, while the next 14 were armed with the longer-ranged SS-N-6 Mod 3, which has two MRV warheads.

Between 1978 and 1987 some 12 Yankee Is had their missile tubes deactivated. Of these 11 were employed as SSNs, and the other as a trials boat for SLCMs. These conversions are intended to keep the Soviet strategic missile force within the SALT II limits as new boats of the Typhoon and Delta IV classes enter service.

The last of the class, which merited the separate designation Yankee II,

Below: Yankee I, the first Soviet SSBN.

Right: Some Yankee Is have been decommissioned.

mounts 12 SS-N-17s. This entered service in 1978 and looks similar to the Delta I, except that the forward edge of its missile casing hump is angled rather than vertical. Like all Soviet boats the Yankees are noisier than their western counterparts and are correspondingly easier to detect.

Class Notes: 34 Yankee Is were built and one Yankee II. Of these, one Yankee I was lost at sea in 1986 and 12 have had their SLBM tubes deactivated. Remaining in the SSBN role are 21 Yankee Is and one Yankee II. One former Yankee I is now serving as the trials boat for the new SLCM system.

Deployment: The relatively short range of the SS-N-6, even in its later versions, means that the Yankees must patrol fairly close to the coast of North America to bring their targets within range. Stark evidence of this was provided in October 1986 when a Yankee I SSBN surfaced after an explosion and fire in its missile compartment. The submarine had been running submerged some 600nm (1,111km) north of Bermuda and 763nm (1,413km) from New York.

Eleven Yankee Is are with the Northern Fleet and 10 with the Pacific Fleet. The sole Yankee II is with the Northern Fleet.

CSS-N-3

Status: In service
Dimensions: Length 32ft 2in (9.8m); diameter 53in (134cm)
Range: 1,512nm (2,800km)
Launch Weight: 33,068lb (15,000kg)
Throw Weight: Unknown
Propulsion: Two stage; solid fuel
Guidance: Inertial
Warhead: One 2MT
CEP: Unknown

Development: China appears to have started development of an SLBM about 1969/70. Some ten years of development elapsed before the first underwater launch of the missile on October 12, 1982 from a Golf-class SSB. This lengthy gestation was due mainly to the need to develop the necessary solid fuel, but the pace equalled that of the development programme for the SSBN.

   Chinese naval missiles are designated 'CSS-N-' by the USA (Chinese, Surface-to-Surface, Naval-) and 'Ju Lang-' (Giant Wave) by the Chinese.

MSBS M-4

Status: In service
Dimensions: Length 36ft 1in (11m); diameter 75.6in (192cm)
Range: 2,376nm (4,400km)
Launch Weight: 79,365lb (36,000kg)
Throw Weight: Unknown
Propulsion: Three stage; solid fuel
Guidance: Inertial
Warhead: Six 150KT MIRV (TN-70)
CEP: Unknown

Development: The series of missiles developed under the designation Mer-Sol Ballistique Stratégique (MSBS) are the fundamental elements of the French strategic nuclear deterrent. The concept was broadly based on that of Polaris, but has been achieved with little non-French help other than the licensing of essential technology. Early test vehicles flew between 1967 and 1970 and led to the MSBS M-1, which entered service in *Le Redoutable* in December 1971. M-1 had a single warhead with a yield of 500KT and a range of 1,296nm (2,400km). This was followed by the M-2 which had a new second stage and a range increased to 1,674nm (3,100km). The M-2 was installed in *Le Foudroyant* during construction and retrofitted to two earlier boats during refits. Next came the M-20, in the course of the 1970s.

   For the second half of the 1980s a completely new missile, the M-4, was developed, which had little in common with the earlier missiles. It could, however, be fitted into the existing submarines, albeit after considerable modification. With a three-stage propulsion system, it mounts six MIRVs, each with a yield of approximately 150KT. These first French MIRVs are stated to be 'extremely precise' and capable of attacking targets over an area of 81x189nm (150x350km). Like the SSBN programme, the development and fielding of an entirely French strategic nuclear missile system is a remarkable achievement.

   The MSBS M-4B is already under development. It will have a range of 2,700nm (5,000km). It will utilise the TN-71 re-entry vehicle.

Deployment: The oldest boat in the fleet, *Le Redoutable,* will retain M-20, but the remaining 4 of the M-20 boats are in the process of being refitted to take M-4, the last refit being completed by 1992. *L'Inflexible* was completed in 1982

CSS-N-1 was the Chinese version of the Soviet SS-N-2a Styx tactical ship-to-ship missile and CSS-N-2, a modified and lengthened derivative; neither were thus strategic missiles.

The CSS-N-3 is a two-stage missile carrying a single warhead estimated to have a yield of between 200KT and 1MT. Believed to be derived from the CSS-4 ICBM, there are 12 CSS-N-3s mounted in two vertical rows of six missiles in each of the Xia class SSBNs. CSS-N-3 is stated to be roughly equivalent in size and performance to the early US Polaris SLBM.

Deployment: 24 missiles in two Xia class SSBNs. Clearly, until a minimum of four boats is available, the Chinese cannot guarantee to have even one boat on operational patrol at any given time.

The most probable deployment areas are in the western Pacific and the China Sea.

Employment: As with the British and the French, China can only provide a retaliatory, counter-value threat to the USSR. However, while the British and French bring second and third decision-making centres into the equation for the threat against the western USSR they are simply out of range of the Soviet Far East. CSS-N-3 brings a second nuclear decision-making centre into Soviet Far Eastern strategic considerations, thus doubtless adding to their feeling of encirclement.

with M-4. By late 1987, strength was 80 M-20 missiles and 16 M-4 missiles. This will progressively change as the refits continue until 1992 when the strength will be 16 M-20s and 80 M-4s. However, the number of warheads will change dramatically, from today's 176 to 496, because of the MIRVs.

The French Navy's deployment problems are reducing as the range of its missiles increases. With the M-1 an SSBN would have had to deploy well into the north-eastern Atlantic to achieve good coverage of the USSR, but the M-4 should enable them to deploy in the western Atlantic.

Employment: The French Navy can, like other smaller nuclear powers such as the UK and China, only manage to threaten a counter-value retaliatory strike against area targets such as cities and large, relatively unprotected industrial or military complexes. The great increase in warheads and in penetration effectiveness should, however, enable the French Navy to have a good chance of getting a reasonable proportion of warheads through to their targets and thus pose a realistic deterrent threat to the USSR.

Below: The MSBS M-4 extends the range of French SLBMs.

Polaris A-3/TK

Status: In service
Dimensions: Length 31ft 6in (9.6m); diameter 54in (137cm)
Range: 2,484nm (4,600km)
Launch Weight: 35,000lb (15,850kg)
Propulsion: Two stage; solid fuel
Guidance: Inertial
Warhead (est.): Three 200KT MRV
CEP: Unknown

Development: The studies which led to the Polaris system began in the USA in 1956, when it became apparent that an advanced solid-propulsion missile to fit submarine launch tubes was a viable proposition. This would permit the missile to be carried much closer to the target and would also enable the launch platform to remain hidden in the depths of the ocean. Polaris A-1 became operational with the first US Navy Fleet Ballistic Missile Submarine (FBMS) in 1960, only five years after the first nuclear-powered submarine, USS *Nautilus*, had made her maiden voyage. In 1962 the first live test of the missile from an operational submarine was a total success. Polaris A-2 had a longer second stage giving increased range and became operational in 1962.

Below: A Royal Navy Polaris missile being test-launched.

Polaris A-3 achieved a 60 percent increase in range by filling the available space more efficiently as well as using a lighter structure and a better propellant. Operational since 1964 it was replaced in the US Navy by Poseidon and now remains in service only with the Royal Navy, in the four boats of the Resolution class.

The Royal Navy's Polaris missiles have always been fitted with a British 'front-end'; ie, the warheads, decoys, penaids and guidance package. A major programme, codenamed Chevaline, was undertaken in the late 1970s and early 1980s to produce a completely new front-end to enable the missile to remain effective through to the end of the century. Few details have been made public and reference books vary in their estimates of Chevaline. The three 200KT MRVs described above seem the most likely configuration. It has been claimed on British TV that the major element in Chevaline's technique is to have made the warheads look like decoys rather than vice versa, as is (not surprisingly) much more usual.

A second programme is being undertaken to replace the rocket motors, which have, quite simply, become too old. This is being undertaken by the original manufacturer in the USA.

Deployment: In the Resolution-class SSBN.

Employment: The only realistic threat that the Royal Navy can pose against the USSR is a second-strike, counter-value attack against major urban and industrial complexes.

Below: A US Polaris is loaded into its launch tube.

Poseidon C-3 (UGM-73)

Status: In service
Dimensions: Length 34ft 1in (10.36m); diameter 74in (188cm)
Range: 2,483nm (4,600km)
Launch Weight: 65,000lb (29,500kg)
Throw Weight: 3,300lb (1,497kg)
Propulsion: Two-stage; solid fuel
Guidance: Inertial
Warhead: Normal load is 10x40KT W-68/Mark 3 MIRVs, plus penetration aids. Maximum load is 14x100KT W-76
CEP: 0.25nm (463m)

Development: Following the successful introduction of Polaris, prolonged studies were made into the benefits of later technology, particularly the introduction of the then new MIRVs. It was also important to seek to extend the range of the missile to enable the SSBN to stand-off further from hostile waters. The resulting missile, Poseidon C-3, was installed in Benjamin Franklin- and Lafayette-class SSBNs, starting with USS *James Madison* (SSBN-627); this latter boat carrying out the first Poseidon deployment on March 31, 1971. Compared with Polaris A-3, Poseidon had at least equal range, carries double the payload and has twice the accuracy, as well as much improved MIRV and penaid capability. A modification programme, begun in 1973 to rectify deficiencies which showed up after it came into service in 1970 was completed in 1978. More than 40 missiles withdrawn from submarines after operational patrols have been test fired, all with excellent results.

Poseidon is currently deployed in the Benjamin Franklin- and Lafayette-class SSBNs. All 31 boats of these two classes were fitted for Poseidon, but 12 were later converted for Trident 1 C-4 leaving 19 with Poseidon, of which a further three have been deactivated to comply with SALT II as Ohio/Trident boats have joined the fleet. Poseidon will, however, serve until well into the 1990s, albeit in gradually diminishing numbers.

Deployment: 619 operational missiles were procured, of which a number have been fired in test flights. The maximum operational requirement now is 16 missiles for each of the remaining 16 SSBNs (256 missiles in all) plus the allot-

Below: A Poseidon missile emerging from the ocean. There is a 40-second interval between launches.

ment for annual testing.

The initial deployment of Poseidon and its comparison with Polaris illustrates the effect of MIRVing. A Polaris SSBN had 16 single warheads, whereas the same boat armed with Poseidon has 160 warheads, which, since they are utilised in the counter-value role, would be used against various different targets.

Employment: The warhead yield and relatively poor CEP mean that Poseidon must be targeted primarily on 'soft' targets such as military airfields, bases, command and communications installations, industrial complexes and urban areas.

Below: The test launch of a Poseidon SLBM, a missile not accurate enough for counter-force missions.

SS-N-6

Status: In service
Dimensions: Length 31ft 8in (9.65m); diameter 64.9in (165cm)
Range: Mod 1/2 — 1,295nm (2,400km); Mod 3 — 1,620nm (3,000km)
Launch Weight: Mod 1/2/3 — 44,000lb (19,958kg)
Throw Weight: Mod 1/2/3 — 1,500lb (680kg)
Propulsion: Two-stage; storable liquid
Guidance: Inertial
Warhead: Mod 1 — 1x1MT; Mod 2 — 1x1MT; Mod 3 — 2x350KT MRV
CEP: Mod 1/2 — 0.55nm (1,020m); Mod 3 — 0.7nm (1,300m)

Development: The third-generation SS-N-6 (Soviet designation: R-21) showed a totally fresh Soviet approach to SLBM design and when it was first seen in a November 1967 parade it posed several problems to Western observers. Geometrically superior to SS-N-5 it has the optimum shape to fill a launch tube. At first thought to have solid-fuel propulsion, it is now believed to have storable liquid fuel, almost certainly N2O4/UDMH. The first stage is large, accounting for almost 75 percent of the launch weight, with four vectored nozzles. There is no cold expulsion device attached to the missile; this must be

SS-N-8

Status: In service
Dimensions: Length 42ft 6in (12.95m); diameter 79in (200cm)
Range: Mod 1 — 4,211nm (7,800km); Mod 3 — 4,913nm (9,100km)
Launch Weight: 45,000lb (20,412kg)
Throw Weight: Mod 1/3 — 1,500lb (680kg)
Propulsion: Two-stage; storable liquid fuel
Guidance: Stellar-Intertial
Warhead: Mod 1 — 1x500KT; Mod 3 — 1x800KT
CEP: Mod 1 — 0.8nm (1,480m); Mod 3 — 0.38nm (900m)

Development: In 1971 this missile began an apparently extremely successful flight-test programme from a single, rebuilt Hotel III SSBN. The SS-N-8 demonstrated a range of some 4,211nm (7,800km), which the then chairman of the US Joint Chiefs of Staff said exceeded by at least 1,620nm (3,000km) the range of any other existing SLBM. It introduced a 'totally new problem' into Western defence planning — and the effect of subsequent tests, when the missile showed ranges exceeding 4,800nm (9,200km), can thus be imagined. SS-N-8 possessed in 1973 a range which the US Navy only equalled in 1979/80.

part of the launch installation in the Yankee 1 class SSBNs which have carried the SS-N-6 since it came into service in 1967.

Three versions of SS-N-6 are known in the West and are believed to be interchangeable. SS-N-6 Mod 1 has a warhead estimated as having approximately 1MT yield. SS-N-6 Mod 2, seen on test in 1972 and deployed from 1973, had improved propulsion, giving a substantial increase in range; US sources have stated that it could hit any part of the USA from the 100 fathom (600ft, 183m) line. Mod 3, which followed closely after Mod 2, has two MRVs which are not independently targetable. According to the US, Mod 3 does not have a hard-target capability. It is estimated that all SS-N-6 now deployed are Mod 3.

Deployment: SS-N-6 is deployed on the 21 remaining Yankee I SSBNs, whose numbers will decrease as more Delta IV and Typhoon SSBNs join the fleet, in accordance with SALT limits.

Employment: This missile is capable of being targeted only against large, soft, area targets such as cities, industrial complexes or major airfields. Limited range compels SSBNs to carry out patrols relatively close to the North American coastline.

Below: The SS-N-6 was the first of the third generation Soviet SLBMs. Here SS-N-6s are seen paraded on the transporters used to take them for quayside launching.

Somewhat larger than SS-N-6, SS-N-8 needed even larger SSBNs — the Delta class — to carry it. They were the largest submarines built up to that time. Even with a hull diameter at least as great as that of the Yankee class, the missile length is such that the launch tubes project above the hull casing, necessitating a whale-back. The Delta I class carried twelve SS-N-8, but the Soviet Navy, determined to match the US Navy's 16-missile submarines, created the Delta II by inserting an extra 55ft (17m) section into the Delta I hull.

A test firing of an SS-N-8 went very wrong in 1986, when an unarmed missile launched from a Delta II SSBN in the Barents Sea and aimed at the missile test range on the Kamchatka Peninsula came down some 1,300nm (2,400km) away, landing near the Amur River on the Sino-Soviet border.

Deployment: A total of 280 missiles are deployed in 18 Soviet Navy Delta I and four Delta II SSBNs. In addition, however, the one Hotel-III SSBN, converted in the 1970s as the trials boat for SS-N-8 and carrying six missiles mounted in the fin, remains in service. One Golf-III SSB, also a trials boat for the SS-N-8, remains in service as well. The grand total of missiles is, thus, 292.

Employment: Large, soft targets, but, in view of warhead yield and CEP may have some capability against protected, but not 'hardened' targets. On-board retargeting using programmed data is possible, as there is only one RV, but a capability for ad hoc retargeting seems unlikely. The very considerable range of SS-N-8 allows the Delta I and II to deploy fairly close to Soviet controlled waters.

SS-N-17

Status: In service
Dimensions: Length 36ft 4in (11.1m); diameter 65in (165cm)
Range: 2,000nm (3,900km)
Launch Weight: Unknown
Throw Weight: 2,500lb (1,134kg)
Propulsion: Two-stage; storable fuel
Guidance: Inertial
Warhead: One 500KT
CEP: 0.75nm (1,400m)

Development: It is indicative of the very lavish amount of money devoted to defence in the USSR that one-off systems are developed and then kept in service for many years in small and very uneconomical numbers. This is the case for the 60 SS-13 ICBMs described elsewhere in this volume, and also for this SS-N-17 naval missile system, which has never been deployed other than in

SS-N-18

Status: In service
Dimensions: Length 46ft 4in (14.1m); diameter 71in (180cm)
Range: Mod 1 — 3,510nm (6,500km); Mod 2 — 4,320nm (8,000km) Mod 3 — 3,510nm (6,500km)
Launch Weight: 74,956lb (34,000kg)
Throw Weight: Unknown
Propulsion: Two-stage; storable liquid fuel
Guidance: Stellar-inertial
Warhead: Mod 1 — 3x500KT (MIRV); Mod 2 — 1x450KT; Mod 3 — 5x500KT (MIRV)
CEP: Mod 1/2/3 — 0.5nm (926m)

Development: SS-N-18 was first seen on test flights only a few weeks after tests had begun on SS-NX-17. It is now fully deployed on Delta III SSBNs and has sufficient range for the submarines to launch the missiles against targets in the USA from the SSBN 'sanctuaries' in the Sea of Okhotsk and the Barents Sea. The original version, SS-N-18 Mod 1, had three 500KT MIRVs, and was the first Soviet MIRVed SLBM. The currently deployed version is the SS-N-18 Mod 3.
Deployment: Delta III SSBNs of the Soviet Navy carry this missile. It is anticipated that the SS-N-23, currently at sea on the Delta IV class, will be fitted in due course to Delta III SSBNs, replacing SS-N-18.
Employment: SS-N-18 Mod 3 has powerful (500KT) MIRVed warheads, but they are not as accurate as those of the US Trident I and II. They are therefore unlikely to have a true counter-force role, although they could be effective against some of the less demanding hard targets.

The major significance of SS-N-18 is its great range, which enables Soviet SSBNs to patrol in areas close to and under the maritime control of the USSR, rather than in the distant waters of the central Atlantic and Pacific Oceans. These areas include the Arctic Ocean.

The SS-N-18 (right) and SS-N-17 (far right) are just two of the SLBMs currently in service with the Soviet fleet, a situation hardly mirrored with the US Navy which operates with just two types aboard their SSBNs. The Soviet missiles also tend to be larger with the SS-N-8, SS-N-18, SS-N-20 and the SS-N-23 all dwarfing the American Poseidon and Trident missiles.

the special Yankee II submarine built specifically to carry it. An alternative possibility is that the missile serves some unique strategic purpose which makes it a cost-effective proposition and, in this context, a single warhead with a post-boost vehicle is certainly unusual (in all other known missile systems a PBV is associated with MIRVs).

SS-N-17 is believed to have been the first Soviet SLBM to use solid propellant and to use a post-boost vehicle. Prototypes were seen on test from land sites in 1975 and testing at sea began in 1977-78 in the specially constructed Yankee II SSBN. Observations of tests have detected the use of only one warhead. So far as is known the SS-N-17 has never been deployed on any other type of submarine, but the type remains in service.

Deployment: Twelve missiles on one single Yankee II SSBN.

Employment: Despite the speculation above, it is not known whether this missile fulfills some special strategic purpose. If it does, then it should be noted that there will be periods when the launch submarine must inevitably undergo refits and the missiles would not be available. Otherwise it can only be assumed that SS-N-17 is simply regarded as another counter-value system, targeted against large, area targets.

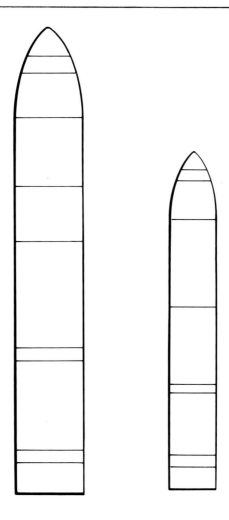

SS-N-20

Status: In service
Dimensions (est.): Length 49ft 2in (15m); diameter 78.7in (200cm)
Range: 4,481nm (8,300km)
Launch Weight: 132,275lb (60,000kg)
Throw Weight: Unknown
Propulsion: Three stage; solid fuel
Guidance: Inertial
Warhead: Six to nine 100KT MIRV
CEP: 0.27nm (500m)

Development: The SS-N-20 was developed for the Typhoon class SSBN, where the launch tubes are uniquely located forward of the fin. It has solid fuel

SS-N-23

Status: In service
Dimensions (est.): Length 46ft 4in (14.1m); diameter 71in (180cm)
Range: 4,480nm (8,300km)
Launch Weight: 88,183lb (40,000kg)
Throw Weight: Unknown
Propulsion: Three stage; storable liquid
Guidance: Inertial
Warhead: Ten 350KT (MIRV)
CEP: 0.48nm (900m)

Development: Somewhat to the surprise of Western naval experts the appearance of the Typhoon/SS-N-20 combination was followed by yet another

Below: An SS-N-23 is launched from amid the arctic ice.

motors, and it is possible that the SS-N-17 served as part of the SS-N-20's development programme.

It is anticipated that the Soviets will begin flight testing of a modified version of SS-N-20 in the near future, with greater accuracy and throw weight than the current version.

Deployment: On board Soviet Navy Typhoon class SSBNs, all of which serve with the Northern Fleet sailing from the new purpose-built submarine base.

Employment: SS-N-20 was designed specifically for the Typhoon class SSBN and its great range coupled with the Typhoon's under-ice capability make it a difficult target. Despite the missile's relative accuracy, the US does not credit the current version of SS-N-20 with a hard-target kill capability, although this is not ruled out for a developed version. It is therefore assumed that SS-N-20 is currently targeted against counter-value targets and some of the less demanding hard targets, particularly in a second-strike context. It is assumed that retargeting is possible prior to launch.

new version of the Delta submarine, Delta IV, with a new type of missile, SS-N-23, which carries ten 350KT MIRVs. It will also be retrofitted into Delta III SSBNs. As with SS-N-20 a modified version can soon be expected with increased range and greater accuracy.

Deployment: Once retrofitted to all 14 Delta IIIs and assuming that the total number of Delta IVs to be built is 10 then there will be 384 SS-N-23 deployed, a total of 3,840 warheads. The latter will comprise about 50 percent of the Soviet Navy's entire warhead strength. SS-N-23 will thus be one of the most important strategic delivery systems in the world.

Delta III has open ocean patrol areas, but Delta IV is capable of under-ice operation.

Employment: SS-N-23 is currently only sufficiently accurate for a counter-value role against area targets or against area military targets, such as airfields. The SS-N-23 Mod 2, expected by the US early in the 1990s, is likely to be very much more accurate and may well have a hard target attack capability.

Below: The Delta IV carries 16 SS-N-23s.

Trident I (C-4) (UGM-96A)

Status: In service
Dimensions: Length 34ft (10.36m); diameter 74in (188cm)
Range: 3,837nm (7,100km)
Launch Weight: 66,035lb (29,954kg)
Throw Weight: 3,000lb (1,361kg)
Propulsion: Three-stage; solid fuel
Guidance: Inertial
Warhead: Eight 100KT W-76/Mark 4 MIRV
CEP: 0.24nm (450m)

Below: The great difference in size between Trident I C-4 (right) and Trident II D-5 (left) can be seen.

Development: Trident I (C-4) was designed to attain 60 percent greater range than Poseidon (C-3). This was achieved by the use of higher energy pro-pellants, the addition of a third-stage motor, and the use of micro-electronics and lighter materials. For example, the equipment section and other missile support structures are made from graphite epoxy and in some cases represent a 40 percent weight saving over alumiuium. A particular innovation was the use of a blunt nose and the nose-mounted 'Aerospike', which deploys on launch to give the same aerodynamic effect as a longer, pointed nose; the blunt nose enables much greater internal volume to be obtained.

Flight testings of Trident I were somewhat shaky at first, but the problems were quickly overcome. Deployment on board converted Lafayette-class SSBNs began in 1979 and on the purpose-built Ohio-class SSBNs in 1981. A total of 630 Trident I missiles have been procured, of which 150 are for opera-tional testing throughout the system's service life.

The British government initially planned to replace their Polaris (A-3/TK) with Trident I (C-4), but later changed to the Trident II (D-5).

Deployment: As of December 31, 1987, operational deployment was 16 ▶

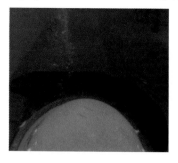

Above: The sequence shows the launch of a Trident I (C-4) SLBM. Here the protective cover has just been opened by remote control from within the hull, revealing the top of the missile transporter capsule.

Above: The gas generator within the launch tube has been activated and the missile has broken through the top of its container. Note the very blunt nose, which contains the Aerospike.

Above: Propelled by gas, the blunt-nose missile shoots toward the surface, passing the submarine's sail, just visible to the left with one of its periscopes extended. This launch is at a depth of 30-40ft (9-12m).

Above: Once clear of the surface the first-stage motor fires, accelerating the Trident I missile on up into space. An Ohio class SSBN would fire its missiles in a ripple over a period of some ten minutes — not simultaneously.

▶ missiles on each of the 12 converted Lafayette/Madison-class SSBNs (192 missiles) and 24 missiles on eight Ohio-class SSBNs (192 missiles). The latter figure will, however, gradually reduce as the submarines are converted to Trident II D-5 between 1991 and 1999.

Deployment of Trident I-armed SSBNs is split between the Pacific and Atlantic Fleets. Two primary deployment benefits result from the Trident I's long-range: home-basing the submarines in the USA and the ability to reach all Soviet targets from the Atlantic, and most, apart from those in the remotest regions, from the Pacific.

Employment: Trident I has little hard target capability, but is capable of attacking moderately hard military bases. Rapid on-boat retargeting is feasible for programmed targets, but the procedure is more lengthy if new coordinates have to be fed in.

Below: A Trident I streaks from the sea.

Trident II (D-5)

Status: In development
Dimensions: Length 45.8ft (13.96m); diameter 74.4in (189cm)
Range: 4,000nm (7,400km) (full load)
Launch Weight: 128,000lb (58,068kg)
Throw Weight: 6,000lb (2,722kg)
Propulsion: Three-stage; solid fuel
Guidance: Stellar-aided inertial; NAVSTAR reception in missile
Warhead: Normal load is ten 475KT W-87/Mark 21 warheads. MaRV warheads are also under consideration
CEP: 0.066nm (122m)

▶

Below: Trident is the mainstay of the USN SSBN fleet.

► **Development:** The Trident II (D-5) has the same diameter as the Trident I, but is 11.8ft (3.6m) longer and will not fit the same launch tubes. It also has virtually double the throw-weight.

The British plan to purchase Trident II, for which four new SSBNs are being built. The British Trident II missiles will have a completely British front-end, to give the UK control over the deployment and targeting of the missiles. However, when announcing their change from Trident I to Trident II it was announced that 'no greater number of warheads would be carried than with Trident I'. This would appear to mean that eight warheads will be carried, rather than 10. The warheads will presumably be developments of the Chevaline fitted to the RN's Polaris A-3/TKs.

Deployment: Planned US deployment is on US Navy Ohio class, SSBNs, joining the Pacific Fleet in 1989 and the Atlantic Fleet in 1992. Current plans call

Below: First flight of the Trident II (D-5) from Cape Canaveral.

for nine SSBNs built from the start for Trident II and for the eight Trident I Ohios to be converted, giving an eventual total of 17 boats with 408 missiles.

Four British SSBNs will carry 16 Trident IIs for a fleet total of 64 missiles. This will, however, increase the British warhead total from the current 192 (assuming three per missile) to 512.

The 4,000nm (7,400km) range of Trident II means that both US and British SSBNs will be able to deploy almost at will in the Pacific and Atlantic Oceans. **Employment:** US Trident II will be capable of attacking hardened targets across the entire spectrum, including ICBM silos and command-and-control facilities. Retargeting will be virtually instantaneous. The front-end of the Royal Navy missiles will be entirely British in design and manufacture; the targeting capability of the British warheads might, therefore, be slightly different.

Below: A diagrammatic view of a Trident II's insides.

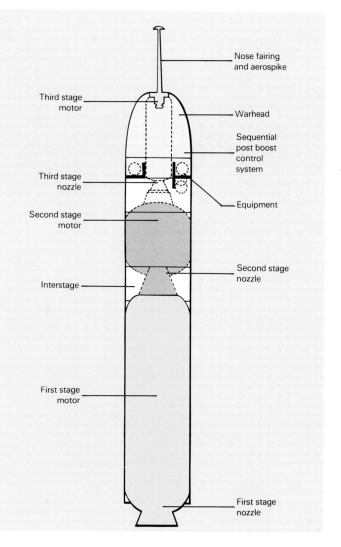

Nose fairing and aerospike

Third stage motor

Warhead

Sequential post boost control system

Third stage nozzle

Equipment

Second stage motor

Second stage nozzle

Interstage

First stage motor

First stage nozzle

The Use of Strategic Weapons in War

Unless he is totally confident that a first-strike will be perfectly successful, it must be a fundamental assumption that a rational aggressor has accepted a retaliatory second strike as the virtually certain consequence of his first strike and believes that he can tolerate the outcome. Herman Kahn, the US nuclear strategist, suggests a 'ladder of escalation' with 44 steps in which Step 21 is nuclear release and Step 44 the holocaust. Any rational aggressor should, therefore, have made a very careful examination of his aims prior to any attack and will also have decided the maximum price he is prepared to pay to achieve that goal. If the aggressor were to set the upper limit at Step 30, escalation by the victim from Step 21 to Step 22 would not affect the aggressor significantly, since he would accept the implications not only of Step 22, but of Steps 23 to 29, as well. The victim's problems is that he is unlikely to know with any degree of certainty what upper limit the aggressor has set to the conflict.

Were the aggressor to be the USSR then she would face a further set of unpredictable factors, due to the existence of nuclear forces in the UK, France and China, which are not only outside US control (although the British force is assigned to NATO) but indepedent of each other, as well. These forces are by no means negligible; it has been stated, for example, that the British force — even when only one boat is at sea — has greater destructive power than all the munitions exploded during World War II. It is difficult to assess just what the USSR thinks of the threat posed by these forces, but it would seem reasonable to conclude that they could not afford to ignore these non-US nuclear forces. On the other hand, the USA needs only to consider the USSR as a potential nuclear adversary, at least in the forseeable future. Nevertheless, in the final analysis, the USA and the USSR are each so powerful that they are the only absolute threats to each other's national survival.

Before undertaking a first strike the aggressor would need to satisfy

Below: Strategic ICBM fields in Continental USA. The USA and USSR know each other's ICBM silo locations to within a matter of feet — hence the switch away from silos to mobile basing.

- ▪ B-1
- ◻ B-52
- ◻ EC/RC-135
- ▪ SR-71
- ◻ FB-111

Malmstrom AFB
Minot AFB
Grand Forks AFB
Ellsworth AFB
Warren AFB
McConnell AFB
Whiteman AFB
Little Rock AFB
Davis Monthan AFB

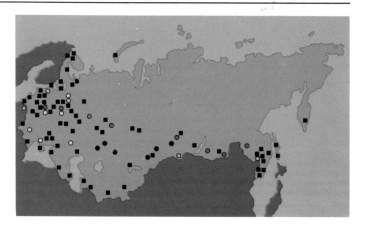

Above: Soviet ICBM sites. The concentration lying in the western USSR is clear, with a second focus in the far East. Such precise maps will become less relevant as rail- and road-mobile systems are deployed.

□ Bomber bases
■ Interceptor bases
◉ SS-11
◉ SS-13
○ SS-17
● SS-18
○ SS-20

himself on some further fundamental points. First, he would need to be sure that his own missile force would function with the reliability and precision predicted from the (necessarily limited) peacetime tests. Secondly, he would need to be sure that the intended victim had neither increased the hardening of his silos nor perfected some new means of neutralising all or some attacking ballistic missiles.

From all this he would need to be reasonably certain that the intended victim would be unable to retain sufficient nuclear retaliatory forces to impose more than the acceptable maximum damage in a second strike. Such a calculation contains so many areas of uncertainty that it would take either a very confident — or an extremely foolhardy — leadership to overcome them.

Second Strike

In terms of retaliating against a first strike, both of the Superpowers face similar problems. The first is that of having a maximum of 30 minutes to make the gravest of all national decisions. The USA is known to designate a 'National Command Authority' (NCA) to make such a decision. It comprises the President, the Secretary of Defense and their duly authorised deputies or successors. Clearly, plans exist to ensure that at least one of these individuals is available within the necessary time. It must be presumed that the USSR has a similar system.

One possible scenario which causes concern in the USA is that of a Soviet first-strike on US ICBM silos, on bombers not on generated alert and with the full peacetime quota of SSBNs in port. According to former

Soviet missile tracking
The current Soviet launch-detection satellite network provides about 30 minutes warning of any US ICBM launch. This is complemented by two over-the-horizon radars directed at US ICBM fields. Eleven Hen House radars at six locations on the USSR's periphery give more detailed information. Five phased-array radars are already in operation with a sixth being built in Siberia.

Launch detection satellites

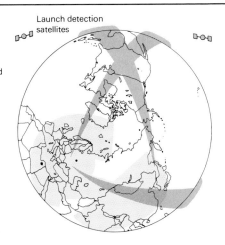

☐ Moscow ABM radars

■ Over-the-horizon radars

☐ New phased-array radars under construction

☐ Hen House radars

Above: The Soviet radar network.

Secretary of Defense, Harold Brown, however, the USA would still 'be able to launch several thousand warheads at targets in the USSR in retaliation. And we would still have the option of withholding a number of these warheads while directing still others to a variety of non-urban targets, including military targets of great value to the Soviet leadership.' Brown's caveat to these remarks is, however, very important: '. . . my assessment is based upon the assumption that the Soviets will remain within the limits set by SALT II.'

The problem of timely decision making in this situation cannot be overestimated. The flight-time of ICBMs between the two Superpowers is some 30 minutes, but if Soviet SSBNs were to be positioned close to the US coastline (and they are, as was shown by the Yankee I accident in 1986) or US SSBNs close to certain areas of the USSR, this warning time could be reduced to between six and 10 minutes.

The attacker's dilemma is that SLBMs could catch soft targets (bomber bases, unhardened military targets) unawares, but currently do not possess the combination of precision and yield necessary to guarantee the destruction of ICBM silos. To launch an attack employing ICBMs, on the other hand, gives greater potential against the silos, but would also give the victim time to launch his

ground alert bombers and also, at least in theory, ICBMs as well.

Both sides rely on a second-strike strategy — that is, they wish to guarantee that, should the enemy strike first, sufficient warheads and delivery vehicles will remain to inflict, in retaliation, more than the acceptable minimum damage to the enemy. The most obvious way to achieve such a second-strike capability is simply to have more nuclear delivery vehicles than the enemy has warheads, the margin of excess being greater than that needed for maximum acceptable retaliatory damage. This strategy leads, of course, to a constant arms race, as both sides would need to maintain numerical superiority to feel safe. It is impractical.

Guaranteeing Survival

There are various other options open to a power wishing to keep nuclear weapons safe from a first strike. Strategic bombers, for example, can be on either airborne or ground alert. The survival of SSBNs is reasonably assured for as long as ASW search techniques are insufficiently developed to give an absolute guarantee of detecting and tracking *all* SSBNs at *all* times throughout their patrol and then to ensure their destruction when required.

ICBMs in silos are, however, a different matter, because they cannot

be hidden; both sides know where the other's silos are to within inches. Only two options seem feasible. The first is 'launch-on-warning', but once launched, missiles cannot be recalled. Alternatively, it could be decided to ride-out the attack, although this presupposes a reasonable knowledge of enemy capabilities, sufficient for confidence that enough missiles would survive; this is the strategy that Harold Brown was referring to in his remarks quoted above.

Nuclear Targeting

Nuclear targeting is, somewhat naturally, a complex business, the first consideration being the capability of missiles, aircraft and warheads. This is not a simple matter of yield, but rather a function of yield and precision. Thus, the fact that the USSR has more ICBMs or greater raw total megatonnage than the USA is not strictly relevant. More important are the number of targets which can be engaged and the Effective Megatonnage (EMT). These indicate firstly the soft target targeting capability — in other words those targets that could be attacked and destroyed with relative ease — and secondly the Counter-Military Potential (CMP), which is a measure of the capability against the hardened targets that require more accurate and/or powerful weapons.

Hardened Counter-Force Targets

Counter-force targets are the enemy's strategic nuclear forces, including politcal and military nuclear command and control centres, and their relevant communications systems. Virtually all of these are hardened and the ability of warheads to destroy them depends upon having a high SSKP. There are, however, practical limits on the hardening that can be achieved. If the SSKP of the weapons increases to a point where the destruction of a silo is virtually guaranteed (there could never be an *absolute* guarantee) then the only option open to the defender is to put his ICBMs on mobile launchers, otherwise his silo-based ICBMs must be a hostage to a first-strike strategy.

Below: MIRVs allow each missile to attack multiple targets.

A counter-force first strike must be targeted on all enemy ICBM silos in the knowledge that if any of those ICBMs are launched-on-warning or launched-under-attack, then the incoming warheads will be wasted on empty silos. For the defence, if they do decide to launch, they must endeavour to identify the empty silos on the aggressor's side, so that they, too, can avoid the same problem of 'cracking' empty silos. On the other hand, if the silos are re-usable (those with cold-launch missiles, for exam-

Below: A Soviet ABM-1B exoatmospheric interceptor.

ple, such as the US Peacekeeper and Soviet SS-17) then clearly they may be worth targeting to prevent their further use.

The only known US unclassified study estimates that high value military targets number some 1,700 in the USSR and 1,300 in the USA. These targets (on both sides) are presumed in most cases to be either extremely hard or, in the case of SSBNs on patrol, difficult to locate.

Soft Counter-Value Targets
Counter-Value targets are cities and industrial complexes. The USA has 162 cities with populations greater

than 100,000, of which 35 complexes exceed one million inhabitants. In contrast, the USSR has 254 cities of over 100,000, but only 13 of these exceed one million. Western Europe has some exceptional concentrations, including eight megalopoli of over 2.5 each million inhabitants each.

For the USA and the USSR, cities are the targets for SLBMs and the less accurate of their ICBMs. Both sides have a credible and survivable second-strike capability and therefore appear to deter each other in this field.

The counter-value threat has been very clearly expounded in a speech to the London Royal United Services Institute by Admiral Sir Ian Easton, Royal Navy: 'The aspect of the Polaris successor issue which I shall concentrate on is the assured independent option which it confers upon the UK to destroy numerous Soviet, cities . . . The nuclear destruction of a number — say, some dozen — of the Soviet cities with a population of over 100,000 would be a traumatic blow to the Soviet Union. Among these cities might be

Below: An extremely accurate US homing-and-kill vehicle.

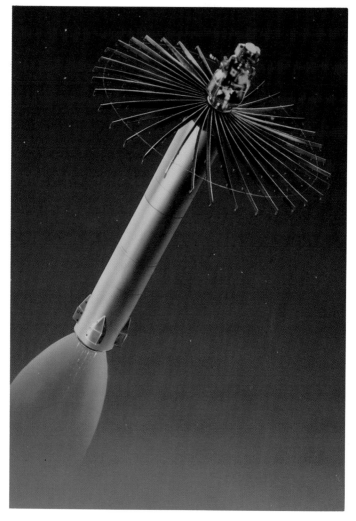

Moscow, Leningrad, Kiev, Kharkov, Gorky and Stalingrad. The enormous loss of population and industry, the disruption of services critical to the life of the country, and the likely destruction of a proportion of the central bureaucracy of a centrally organised state, could be expected to markedly weaken the vitality of the nation and the will of its people, and, perhaps, of its armies.'

Other Military Targets

There is a further category of low collateral damage, high value military targets, which for convenience and to avoid confusion with strategic nuclear forces are referred to as 'Other Military targets' (OMT). These are estimated to number some 2 to 3,000 in the USSR and 1,000 in the USA.

Both the USA and USSR are known to devote considerable attention to detailed analyses of potential targets, with a view to discovering the really important critical points and, in a nuclear conflict, destroying them in order to dislocate the entire system.

Other Uses of Strategic Weapons

Some strategic weapons which count against the deployed total are known to be used for other purposes, although the details are little publicised. The USA, for example, has a system called the Emergency Rocket Communications System (ERS), which is installed on eight Minuteman II ICBMs at Whiteman AFB in place of their warheads. The USSR may have similar systems, although no details are known, but they have admitted to another use in allocating some of their ICBMs to 'navy groupings at sea'. The large yield of some of the Soviet ICBMs would cause destruction over a large area of ocean and make them suitable, under certain circumstances, for use against groups of hostile SSBNs.

Right: A US Defense Support Program Satellite. This satellite monitors Soviet and other missile tests and would detect a nuclear attack.

Siting Strategic Weapons

The siting of strategic weapons has been the subject of the most stringent and detailed studies by all nations possessing them. Among the major factors to be considered are that the weapons must be in the right place to undertake their assigned mission when called upon to do so, they must be physically secure against pre-emptive strike by a hostile power and, of increasing importance, at least in the West, they must cause minimal interference to the environment. The siting must also be politically acceptable and the individual elements of the system (in particular the launchers) must be under central control. Each of the major options — ICBM, SLBM and bombers — has advantages and disadvantages in these spheres.

The SSBN/SLBM combination is in many ways the nearest to the ideal. They have siting flexibility in that they can move around the oceans, they are very secure under normal circumstances, and they have minimal public and environmental impact. However, they have one major problem in that communications between the authorities ashore and submerged SSBNs is inherently difficult, as described on page 97. There also may be problems for SSBNs in the future as Anit-Submarine Warfare (ASW) techniques become more effective.

For bombers the siting of airfields is not a major problem and modern aircraft, such as the US B-1B and the Soviet Blackjack, have sufficient combination of internal tankage and in-flight refuelling support to make range a minor problem. The bomber's problem lies in getting through to its target despite the opponent's air defence systems — not where its airfield is sited.

ICBM Siting

The major siting difficulties have always arisen concerning the land-based missiles — ICBMs. The ICBM has, to a large extent, become a vic-

tim of its own success. So long as its only effective enemy was the relatively slow-flying manned bomber the missile could be defended by air-defence systems and basing was not a critical issue; it is only since the ICBMs have become so accurate that they can attack opponent's individual ICBMs in their silos that defensive siting has become so important. This process has been clearly seen in the USA where the Atlas ICBM, deployed between 1960 and 1967, was initially sited in soft-skinned, above-ground garages which featured end-sliding roofs to allow the missile to be erected for propellant loading and launch. When the Soviets developed ICBMs which threatened this system the Atlas was placed in enormous silos, sitting on an elevating launch platform which was raised to the surface for launch. Next came Titan, which sat in a silo

Left: The SSBN is able to hide in the depths of the ocean.

Above: ICBM silos are increasingly vulnerable.

hardened to withstand the unprecedented overpressure of 300psi (21kg/cm²). Titan I was, like Atlas, raised to the surface for launch, but Titan II was designed to be launched from within its silo, which had a mighty W-shaped flame deflector at the base leading to sloping exhaust ducts. From here onwards silo technology has concentrated on ever harder structures, with all US silos how hardened to about 2,000psi (140kg/cm²). Some Soviet silos reach the almost incredible figure of 5,000psi (350kg/cm²).

The USA and the USSR have both sought ways to escape from this situation, and both have examined a whole series of mobile bases for their ICBMs. The Soviet SS-16 bedevilled the arms reduction talks in the 1970s. It was reported to be an SS-20 with an additional stage to give full ICBM range, and mounted on a mobile

launcher. SS-16 was not, in the event, deployed and the Soviet ICBMs of that generation (SS-17, -18 and -19) were all placed in silos. However, the next generation of Soviet ICBMs are both mobile (SS-24 by rail and SS-25 on wheeled launchers) as, it now appears, will be the later US Peacekeepers and SICBM.

The USA, however, has examined numerous other siting options, particularly in the gap before the full deployment of Peacemaker. 'Continuous Patrol Aircraft' (CPA) was a scheme to deploy ICBMs on large, fuel-efficient aircraft capable of staying aloft for protracted periods, with other elements of the force on alert at airfields. The key element of this concept was that the missile had to be dropped from the aircraft and then launched while descending by parachute. Trials were carried out with the Lockheed C-5 aircraft and Minuteman missiles, and the concept was proved to be workable. A great advantage of this scheme was that it was difficult to locate and attack the aircraft in a pre-emptive strike, but its weakness lay in the vulnerability of the airfields. Air launch also made the missile less accurate.

Multiple Protective Structure (MPS) bases consisted of 200 tracks of about 25 miles (40km) circumference, each equipped with 23 shelters and one ICBM: these would have been located in Utah and Wyoming. The idea was that the 200 missiles (and decoys) could be moved around the 'racetrack' in a random fashion on large, wheeled Transporter-Erector-Launchers (TEL). A variation of this scheme also involved 200 missiles, but in this case moving between no less than 4,600 shelters spread over an area of 5,000 square miles (12,800km²). Various schemes of moving the missiles were also considered. Above-ground wheeled TFLs was one option, while another was that the race tracks would be shallow tunnels and that to fire, the TFL would halt and then raise its missile through the tunnel roof; one such 'break-out' test was successfully carried out in September 1978.

Deep Basing (DB) involved placing ICBMs either singly or in groups deep

Below: A US Peacekeeper is cold launched from its silo.

underground where they would ride out an attack and then emerge to carry out a retaliatory strike. One of the major DB schemes was the 'Mesa concept' in which the missiles, crews and the equipment necessary to break-out through the earth were to be placed in interconnected tunnels some 2-3,000ft (610-914m) deep under a mesa or similar geological formation. The scheme's disadvantages lay in its poor reaction time, its ability only to launch after an attack, and the difficulty it posed for arms

Above: A full-scale mock-up of one version of the US Small ICBM sometimes called Midgetman.

control verification, even supposing that digging-out all the launcher equipment had proved feasible.

Closely-Based Spacing (CBS) (also known as 'Dense pack') was considered, too. In current missile

Below: An artist's impression of the Small ICBM (SICB) mobile launcher.

fields individual silos are spaced sufficiently far apart to ensure that not more than one can be destroyed by one incoming warhead. Dense Pack proposed to take the opposite approach and to site 100 MX missiles in superhardened silos deliberately placed close together. The idea was that this would take advantage of the 'fratricide' effect in which incoming warheads would be deflected or destroyed by the nuclear explosions of the preceding warheads. The distance between individual silos was to have been sufficient to ensure that more than one could not have been destroyed by one warhead, but small enough to ensure that fratricide occurred — in a distance of the order of 1,800ft (549m) was suggested. The USAF claimed that some 50 to 70 percent of the missiles would have survived.

Yet another scheme to have been considered was placing waterproofed ICBMs in the sea, being deployed either by ships or aircraft and launched on orders from the shore. This was actually tested and proved feasible in the US Navy's Project Hydra in the 1960s. All that was required was the waterproofing of the vehicle, a flotation collar (jettisoned on launch) and the necessary electronics for remote arming and launch. On the firing of the first stage motor the water becomes, in effect, the launch-pad and the missile lifts off for a normal flight, as does an SLBM.

Above: A further basing mode is in 'rail garrisons' where missiles can be dispersed along tracks.

Below: The Boeing-Goodyear Hard Mobile Launcher Mobility Test-Bed was delivered to the USAF in 1985. The USSR has had such systems deployed for several years.

Support Systems

A vital factor in all strategic nuclear systems is C^3 (Command, control and communications) which confers the ability to control and coordinate their strategic forces, enables them to receive timely and accurate information upon which to base their decisions, and, finally, gives them the ability to pass nuclear release messages in an effective fashion. In terms of strategy, this raises an interesting dilemma, in that any potential enemy may, on the one hand wish to cut his opponent's strategic communications to cause the maximum confusion and delay. On the other hand, such disruption could well prevent the other side from controlling its subordinates, thus leading to lower echelons acting in an illogical and unpredictable manner.

A further consideration is the increasing vulnerability of satellite C^3 systems. The ability to 'take-out'

communications satellites undoubtedly exists on both sides, and there may be strong military pressure to destroy some, perhaps even all of an opponent's satellites in a preemptive attack. However, the destruction of space-based early warning, reconnaissance or communications systems could only be construed as a major escalation, with a nuclear strike virtually the only effective, or even credible, response.

US Strategic C^3

The US command system is based upon the person of the President of the United States and his duly authorised deputies or successors. The President is always accompanied by a uniformed officer carrying the equipment necessary to inform the President of an incoming attack and to enable him to transmit his response. All envisaged reactions are embodied in a document known as

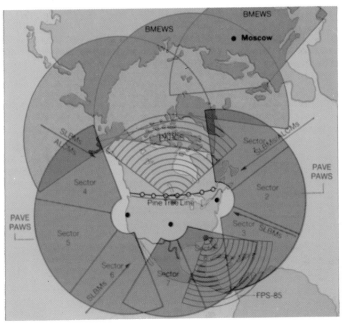

the 'Single Integrated Operational Plan' (SIOP), but the authorizing messages must be passed from the President down through the chain-of-command to the individual officers controlling the actual weapons at the missile silo, the submarine control room or in the aircraft cockpit.

To achieve this, the first link in the chain is the National Military Command Centre (NMCC) in the Pentagon in Washington DC, which is 'shadowed' by the Alternate NMCC at Fort Richie, Maryland, and by the National Emergency Airborne Command Post (NEACP). The latter is provided by six Boeing E-4B aircraft of the USAF, based on the Boeing 747 civilian airliner, each of which has now cost in excess of $50 million. These are designed to carry out the vital role of providing the nation's seat of executive authority in time of extreme crisis or all-out war and are able to command the USAF and USN

strategic retaliatory forces. They are also as secure as is possible against EMP, radiation and other nuclear effects.

These aircraft are packed with special communications operating on frequencies ranging from VLF/LF for communicating to submerged submarines (for which they deploy a trailing wire antenna some 5,000ft (1,524m) long), up to UHF and SHF (using antennae inside the dorsal 'doghouse' fairing). The aircraft are in contact with the Defense Satellite Communications System (DSCS-III) and also have down-links to a variety of ground-based military communications systems. The aircraft are fitted with the Improved Airborne Launch Control System (IALCS) which allows on-board launch and, if required, the subsequent retargeting of Minuteman and Peacekeeper missiles.

A crew of 94 is carried on the

Left: The US ballistic missile warning system includes the facilities shown here and bases in Australia and Guam.

Below: Distant and Early Warning (DEW) radar sites in Greenland are vital for American security.

Above: Lockheed EC-130 TACAMO aircraft are on constant patrol as part of the system to guarantee communications to SSBNs.

Left: The operations area inside a TACAMO aircraft. Communications to submerged SSBNs are by Very Low Frequency (VLF) signals.

4,620sq ft (429.2m²) main deck, of each of these aircraft. This deck is divided into five operating areas: the NCA area (the National Command Authority is the body that will make the decision to launch nuclear attacks. Effectively, it is the President and the Secretary of Defense), conference room, briefing room, battle staff compartment (26 people) and communications control centre (15 people). One aircraft is aloft at all times, commanded by a general officer, and every mission is potentially 'live'. The principal base of the NEACP force is Offutt AFB, Nebraska; if it was necessary to pick up the President, then it is most likely that

one of these aircraft would land at Andrews AFB, the nearest base to Washington, DC.

Next in the US strategic chain are the subordinate commands, including Strategic Air Command (controlling the bombers and ICBMs), and the Pacific and Atlantic Fleets (controlling the SSBN/SLBM force). These, too, have main headquarters and alternative centres on the ground, and are backed up by airborne command posts, similar to the NEACP described above, but mounted in Boeing EC-135 aircraft and with correspondingly smaller staffs. One example is the SAC Post-Attack Command and Control Systems (PACCS), known as the 'Looking Glass' mission, which is mounted in EC-135As, one of which has always been airborne since February 3, 1961. This involves three aircraft per day, each flight lasting a minimum of eight hours. The task commander, designated Airborne Emergency Actions Officer (AEAO), is a general officer from SAC, assisted by battle staff, communicators, technicians and the

flight crew. There is a UHF link to the Air Force Satellite Communications System (AFSATCOM) and there are numerous down-links to SAC's underground HQs, HQs 8th and 15th Air Forces, airfields, other aircraft on ground and airborne alert and ICBM launch control centres.

Low-data-rate communications to US strategic forces and two-way teletype communications for strategic force management are provided by the AFSATCOM system, in which UHF transponders are carried 'piggyback' on other 'host' satellites such as the USN Fleet Satellite Communications System (FLTSAT-COM). Ground terminals are widely distributed.

DSCS-III satellites use both SHF and UHF to increase resistance to jamming and are used to pass high-data-rate missile attack warnings and other infromation from the satellite early warning system to command centres and also to provide a further link between the E-4B NEACPs and the strategic forces. Further com-munications will be provided by the Military Strategic and Tactical Relay (MILSTAR) satellite system. These satellites, currently in full development, use EHF links and incorporate defensive measures intended to en-sure their availability in any nuclear war. They will be used to provide two-way links between various com-manders and their forces.

Just entering service with the US is the Ground-Wave Emergency Network (GWEN), which provides an EMP-resistant communications system to carry warning data to the NCA and retaliatory orders from the NCA to the strategic forces.

The World-Wide Military Command and Control System (WM-MCCS) is designed to provide strategic communications plus data processing and display facilities to NCA and subordinate commands; among other facilities, it gives force location and status information. In the late 1970s some spectacular failures by WMMCCS, leading to er-roneous (and well-publicised) 'alerts',

gave it degree of notoriety, but these problems seem now to have been overcome.

Currently in development is the Miniature Receiver Terminal (MRT), which will be used by airborne strategic bombers to receive low-data-rate messages at Very Low Frequency/(VLF). Despite limitations in message-handling capacity, the USAF considers that the greater ranges possible with VLF, and its inherent ability to resist nuclear weapons effects make it a valuable addition to their C[3] facilities. This is the first known application of VLF in aircraft.

Yet further communications stand-by is provided by the Emergency Rocket Communications System (ERCS). This consists of eight Minuteman II ICBMs, in which the warhead has been replaced by communications equipment, which will provide an effective, if somewhat short-lived, radio relay between the NCA and SSBNs, should the need arise.

Communicating with SSBNs

The mobility of SSBNs and their ability to hide themselves in the depths of the oceans creates a major C[3] problem: the provision of reliable communications. Sea water attenuates virtually all radio transmissions, such attenuation increasing with both the depth of the receiving antenna and the frequency of the signal. Thus, to receive signals on the HF band or higher the submarine must either be on the surface, deploy a mast-mounted antenna from shallow submerged depth, or deploy an antenna buoy from slightly greater depth. But such forays near the surface are inherently dangerous, since they lay the submarine open to detection and subsequent attack.

Very Low Frequency (3-30KHz) signals, however, can penetrate to a depth of some 10ft (3m) beneath the surface and are already used for passing Loran-C navigation information

Below: The Boeing E-4 AABNCP carries a large battle staff.

and naval broadcast signals. To achieve long-range communications at greater depths it is necessary to resort to an Extremely Low Frequency (ELF, 300Hz-3KHz) system, with which signals can be received down to about 330ft (100m), or possibly even deeper. Such a system is very expensive mainly because of the great length of the antennas: the US 'Austere ELF' system, for example, will have an antenna some 124 miles (200km) long, while the more sophisticated and survivable systems once projected would have had antennas covering an area of some 17,000km²! ELF suffers from the inevitable natural noise and also has a very low-data-rate. Again, the US 'Austere ELF' system, for example, would have been capable of passing just one three-letter group in 15 minutes, although it is reported that using a compressed code analogous to flag-signalling some 17,500 different messages could be passed using just three letter groups. Perhaps the most important use of ELF, however, would be to act as a 'bell-ringer' by instructing the submerged SSBN to approach the surface and deploy a float- or mast-mounted antenna to receive an HF or satellite signal.

Above: NORAD HQ inside Cheyenne Mountain, Colorado, a complex vital to US war plans.

Right: The Washington terminal of the US-Soviet 'hotline'.

The primary means of communicating to SSBNs, however, is the TACAMO (TAke Charge And Move Out) system, which uses a fleet of aircraft, two of which are always airborne, one over the Atlantic, the other over the Pacific, with others at 15 minutes ground alert. The aircraft fly 10½ hour missions, starting at one airfield and ending at another, all in a random pattern to mislead potentially hostile observers. The TACAMO aircraft can receive signals from FLTSATCOM, AFSATCOM, the NEACP, the airborne Fleet command posts, and a variety of ground stations. The principal down-link to submerged SSBNs is by Very Low Frequency (VLF), using a 6.2 mile (10km) trailing wire antenna and a 100KW transmitter. When required to transmit, the aircraft banks in a continuous tight circle which results in the antenna hanging vertically below. The aircraft, in addition to its VLF downlink to the SSBN also has

Low Frequency and High Frequency transmitters.

The current TACAMO fleet comprises four Lockheed EC-130G and 16 EC-130Q, the latter having improved equipment and crew accommodation. These are being replaced over the period 1987-1991, due not only to the age of the current fleet, but also to the much greater coverage needed for Trident submarines. The new aircraft are 15 Boeing EC-6As, which use the E-3A AWACS airframe, but without the rotodome. They are equipped with the Airborne Very Low Frequency (AVLF) communications fit, an on-board generating station with sufficient power to give a radiated signal of some 200KW, a reel-wound 2.5 mile (4km) steel wire antenna, and a very sophisticated ESM suite. They are EMP-hardened. The role and mission-profile remain much as they are for the EC-130, however, and they will also carry a similar variety of up- and down-links.

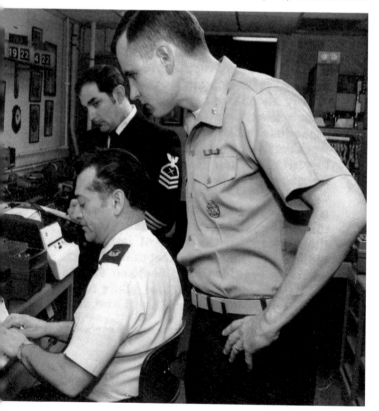

Strategic Defence

US Defences

There is nothing new in constructing defences against ballistic missiles. Both the USA and USSR deployed ABM systems in the early 1970s, using nuclear-armed missiles controlled from the ground. The US 'Safeguard' system was sited in North Dakota to protect two ICBM fields, while the Soviet Galosh system protected the Soviet capital, Moscow. Considerable reservations about effectiveness led to the abandonment of the US system in 1976, but the Soviets kept theirs and have continued to upgrade it.

Having accepted the premise that the opponent must move first by launching his missiles first, possibly attacking with over a thousand missiles fired from both ground sites and submarines, then the most effective time to counter-attack them is during the boost phase, since there are many fewer targets — and virtually no decoys — to be destroyed than after the MRVs or MIRVs have been deployed. Launch detection is already a mature technology and detection sufficient for boost-phase interception is currently feasible. Once in the post-boost and midcourse phase target tracking is complicated by the presence of decoys, dummies, chaff and other devices, but various devices are now in development, such as long wavelength infra-red phased-array microwave radars and ultra-violet laser radars, which might be space-, aircraft- or ground-based. During reentry, finding the right target is less difficult, mainly because decoys and debris behave differently from RVs, but interceptor vehicles must be extremely fast to carry out effective attacks on incoming warheads.

There are a number of US ballistic missile warning systems. In outline, the detection and tracking process would start with the Satellite Early Warning System (SEWS), consisting of one satellite over each of the Atlantic, Pacific and Indian Oceans; these can sense Soviet ICBM launches within 90 seconds and pass instantaneous alerts to their control and tracking ground stations at Guam (in

Below: The Soviet Gazelle ABM is being used to update Moscow's defences.

Right: The USA has plenty of radars, such as this PAVE PAWS, but no ABMs.

the Western Pacific), Nurrungar (near Alice Springs, Australia) and Pine Gap. The Ballistic Missile Early Warning System (BMEWS) would then take over, utilising its ground stations at Clear (Alaska), Thule (Greenland) and Fylingdales Moor (United KIngdom) to track and identify the missiles.

Closer in to the USA the Perimeter Acquisition Radar Attack Characterisation System (PARCS), located at Grand Forks, North Dakota, can identify the number of RVs and predict the impact sites for incoming targets within its north-facing, 130-degree arc and 1,350nm (2,500km) range. Satellites and the first two PAVE PAWS phased-array sites in Massachusetts and California warn of SLBM and ALCM attack from east and west respectively. The FPS-85 site in Florida would continue to watch the southern approaches, particularly for FOBS attack, although it will deactivate when the final two PAVE PAWS sites in Georgia and Texas have been completed. The USN Space Surveillance System (NAVSPASUR) stretches across the southern USA, with nine field stations, three transmitting and six receiving.

Soviet Defences

Less is known about the Soviet early warning and defensive systems, but the major difference between the two is that the USSR has deployed an ABM system and the USA does not currently have one. Like the USA, the Soviets make extensive use of satellites for early warning and target tracking, and have, among others, nine in highly elliptical, semi-synchronous orbits, with ICBM/SLBM launch detection capability. These are supported by three Over-the-Horizon-Backscatter (OTH-B) radars: one each at Minsk and Nikolayev in the Caucasus covering the US and polar areas, and a third at Nikolayev-na-Amur covering China; the former two are estimated to give 30 minutes warning of the launch of ICBMs from the US missile fields. The next layer consists of eleven, well-established Hen House radars,

with 3,240nm (6,000km) ranges, located at six sites covering targets incoming from the west, south-west, north-east, south-east and south. These confirm the satellite and OTH-B warnings, determine the size of an attack and provide target-tracking data.

The USSR is currently in the process of deploying a series of nine new Long-Range Phased-Array Radars (LPAR), which, when completed in the mid-1990s, will provide significantly improved target-tracking and handling capabilities, replacing the Hen House system. The three western LPARs, at Lyaki, Mishelevka, Pechora and Sary-Shagan.

There has been some argument over the Krasnoyarsk radar. In signing the ABM Treaty in 1972 the USSR and USA acknowledged the need for ballistic missile early warning radars, while seeking to prevent their use in a nationwide ABM system. The treaty restricts the deployment of new radars. They can only be placed on the periphery of national territory and oriented outwards. The USSR say that the Krasnoyarsk installation is designed for space-tracking and now for ballistic-missile early warning and does not violate the treaty. The USA, on the other hand, argues that the Krasnoyarsk radar does violate the treaty, firstly because it is located deep within the USSR, some 405nm (750km) from the Mongolian border. Secondly, argues the USA, it is not pointing outwards — and certainly not towards the nearest (Mongolian) border, but eastwards across Soviet territory.

Soviet Anti-Ballistic Missile Defences

The 1972 ABM Treaty permitted a total of 100 ABM launchers and for many years the USSR had a system of 64 ABM-1B Galosh launchers at sites around Moscow. In 1980 these began to be run down. By 1987 there were 16 launchers. The Galosh system comprises two large battle management radars, known as Dog House and Cat House, located south of Moscow, and four firing complexes, each with Try Add tracking and guidance radars and four above-ground, reloadable launchers. The

Above: Future Soviet defences will include ASATs (top) and ground-based lasers.

Right: Four PAVE PAWS radars are sited around the US.

Galosh missile itself has a 3MT nuclear warhead and is designed for exoatmospheric interception of RVs (that is it aims to strike before the RVs re-enter the Earth's atmosphere).

A new Moscow ABM system will provide a two-layer defence, comprising a new, improved, silo-based version of Galosh, (designated SH-04) combined with the SH-08 Gazelle, a very high acceleration, endoatmospheric missile (designed to intercept RVs within the atmosphere). New radars have been built for the system, including the huge Pill Box installation at Pushkino north of Moscow. This modernization programme will bring the Soviet active ABM defences up to the 100 permitted by the ABM Treaty.

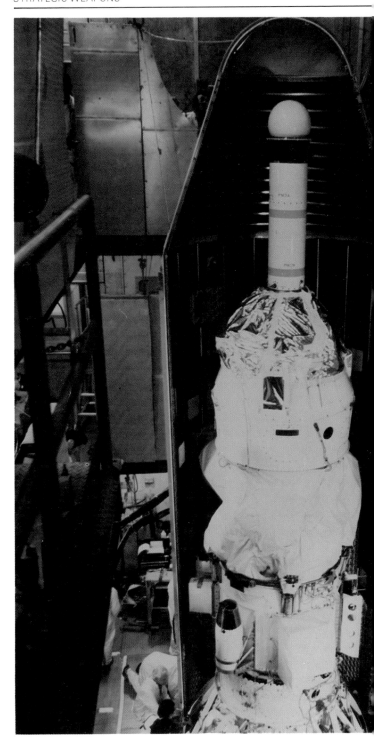

US Defence Against Strategic Bombers and ALCMs

The threat to North America from manned bombers has existed since the mid-1950s, but dealing with this particular threat has never been given the priority or resources made available to other areas. However, the rapid increase in Soviet ALCMs and the deployment of Blackjack bombers caused a major re-examination in 1987. The first early-warning layer lies in the various satellite systems, but these are now complemented by airborne and ground radar systems.

Long-range ground-based detection uses the new Over-the-Horizon-Backscatter (OTH-B) radars. The first chain of three radars in Maine is already operational, a second chain is being built in Oregon and two more are being planned, one to be located somewhere in the south and the other in Alaska. Each chain comprises three sites, each covering an arc of approximately 60 degrees (ie, 180 degrees in all) over a range bracket of 486nm (900km) to 2,052nm (3,800km).

OTH-B radars can provide long-range surveillance to the east, west and south, but their capability is limited when looking north because of ionospheric disturbances caused by the Aurora Borealis; thus, a different technological solution is required. For many years the Distant Early Warning (DEW) Line system of manned sites spread across the north from Alaska, through Canada to Greenland provided warning of aircraft coming across the polar routes. This is now obsolete, but it is being replaced by the North Warning System (NWS), which will consist of a series of radars on a line roughly following the 70 degree north parallel. The system will consist of 13 long-range, low-maintenance, AN/FPS-117 Seek Igloo automated radars, which have already been procured. These do not, however, give fully comprehensive cover and a further 39 short-range (60-81nm — 110-

Left: This SDI payload is a Hughes Phoenix missile sensor, which guided two space vehicles to an intercept.

150km), unmanned radars are needed to fill in the gaps in low-level coverage. There will eventually be some 33 sites: thirteen in Alaska, thirteen in Canada, four in Greenland, two in Iceland and one in Scotland.

The air forces allocated to defend North American airspace against bomber and ALCM attack are thin, to put it mildly. The USAF interceptor force currently comprises 15 squadrons (four active, eleven Air National Guard), which maintain a ground alert at US airfields. In periods of tension these forces would be brought to a higher state of alert, dispersed and reinforced by other available aircraft. In peacetime their mission is to intercept and identify unknown aircraft approaching North American airspace. In war they would provide a defence against bombers and ALCM which even Secretary of Defense Weinberger described as 'limited'.

The active USAF aircraft currently assigned to this mission comprise three squadrons with the McDonnell Douglas F-15 Eagle (58 aircraft) and one squadron with the General Dynamics F-106 Delta Dart (18 aircraft), an extremely elderly type which entered service in 1959! These are complemented by eleven ANG (Air National Guard) squadrons: seven with the McDonnell Douglas F-4 Phantom (126 aircraft); one with the F-15 (18 aircraft); and three with the F-106 (54 aircraft) — a grand total of 292 aircraft. (To this must be added the Canadian contribution of two squadrons of CF-18 in the air defence role.) The US's current plans call for the disbandment of the fourth active (F-106-equipped) squadron as a 'cost-saving measure' and the re-equipment of the ANG squadons with a new aircraft of a type yet to be decided.

Soviet Defences Against Manned Bombers and ALCMs

The Russian people have been obsessed with the security of their homeland since Napoleon's invasion of 1812 and the subsequent attacks in 1914 and 1941. It is, therefore, hardly surprising that they should make strenuous efforts and commit enormous resources to defence against air attack. The seriousness with which they regard intrusions was exhibited by their shooting down of a Korean Air Lines Boeing 707 in 1978, when the aircraft strayed into Soviet airspace near Murmansk, where it was shot down by a Sukhoi Su-15 interceptor; two passengers were killed but the aircraft crash-landed on a frozen lake and the remainder survived. In a further incident a Boeing 747, somewhat astonishingly of the same airline, was shot down on September 1, 1983 with the loss of all aboard. The intrusion of a young West German in a civilian light aircraft in 1987, however, was so ineptly handled that he was able to land in Red Square and numerous senior officers had to be disciplined as a result.

Defences against manned aircraft have made enormous strides since the Tallinn Line was set up along the western boundary of the USSR in the mid-1950s. Today the air defence system has been improved in terms of the quantity and quality of radars deployed along the entire western border from Murmansk in the north to the Turkish border; depth has also been added with particular emphasis on the Moscow-Leningrad area and Baku.

Early warning, tracking and target designation are given by a huge network of some 10,000 ground-based radars of a variety of types. These give virtually complete coverage of the USSR at medium-to-high altitudes, but are not so comprehensive at low level. This gap is, however, being filled gradually by an ever-expanding force of AWACS aircraft, currently some seven Tupolev Tu-126 Moss aircraft, and now being reinforced by a growing number (four: 1987) of Ilyushin Il-76 Mainstay (previously known as SUAWACS). An air-to-air refuelling version of the Ilyushin Il-76 (designated Midas by NATO) is also being deployed to support both strategic bombers as well as the AWACS and AD forces.

There are some 9,000 strategic SAM launchers and nearly 5,000 tactical SAM launchers (excluding hand-held types). Five strategic systems (the elderly SA-1, SA-2, SA-3 and SA-5, and the much more modern SA-10) are operational, with a brand-new system — SA-12B —

about to enter service. SA-1, -2,-3 and -5 have been in service for many years and have been tested operationally in Vietnam and the Middle East. The first three are unlikely to pose too great a threat (except in sheer numbers), but the SA-5 has been repeatedly updated, showing continuing Soviet faith in the system. SA-10 came into service in 1980 and has multi-target handling and engagement capabilities; it is considered capable of intercepting aircraft at all heights, can cope with low-altitude/small radar cross-section aircraft, such as cruise missiles, and also has some potential against tactical ballistic missiles. Over 80 sites are now operational (with another 20 under construction), the majority being near Moscow, suggesting that SA-10's primary mission is the terminal defence of key leadership, military and industrial installations. The SA-12 system is capable of intercepting aircraft at all altitudes as well as cruise missiles and tactical ballistic missiles, while the SA-12B may also have a capability against some types of strategic ballistic missiles.

Some 2,250 interceptors are employed by the Air Defence Troops (VPVO) in the stratégic air defence role, and many of these planes have an all-weather capability. The most important types are the very modern MiG-29 Fulcrum (58 aircraft), MiG-31 Foxhound (150) and Su-27 Flanker, supported by the somewhat older MiG-23 Flogger B/G (430), MiG-25 Foxbat E (300), Sukhoi Su-15 Flagon E/F (200), Yak-28P Firebar (90) and Tu-28 Fiddler B (90). (All these figures are approximate.) An additional 2,000-odd interceptors could be diverted to the air defence role, if considered necessary. The most capable of these is the MiG-31 which has a lookdown/shootdown and multiple-target engagement capability, although, as is usual in the USSR, it is not being entrusted with this task alone but is complemented by the equally advanced and capable MiG-29 and Su-27.

Below: These photographs show the test carried out by the Hughes Phoenix missile sensor shown on pages 104-105. In No. 1 only one vehicle is visible. In No. 2 the second vehicle is approaching. No. 3 is just prior to impact. No. 4 shows the moment of impact.

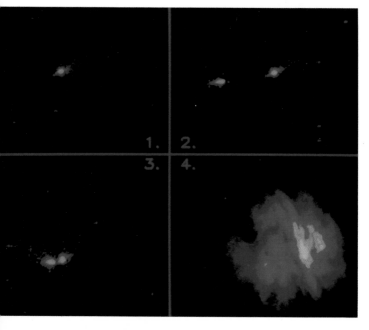

Assessing the Nuclear Balance

There is an understandable tendency to look for a balance sheet in the strategic arms issue. Many countries, but especially the USA and the USSR, are spending vast sums on these weapons systems and it is natural that some people should ask whether they are getting their money's worth, and others, whether one side or another is ahead or behind in the 'arms race'. This leads to a requirement for an assessment of the weapons, the systems and the controlling apparatus and a comparison between the two, but it is here that the difficulties start. Part of the problem lies with security — for the US and the USSR these are matters which concern their national survival — but it also involves the sheer difficulty of placing systems in such a relationship to each other that objective comparisons can be made. Raw data is of little relevance: it means little for example, that the USA has 640 SLBMs and the USSR 944. SLBMs do not attack each other and there is thus no immediate significance in the direct ratio of one side's SLBMs to the other's.

Intelligence

There is a remarkable amount of information available if one has the time to track it down and the knowledge of where it might be; it emerges in many places from specialist journals to the Minutes of US Congressional Committees, from glossy brochures issued at defence industries shows to TV newscasts, and in the 'background briefings' associated with disarmament talks. One major factor is that because Soviet security is so strict, a great proportion of the information on their strategic weapons systems comes from the USA. But while the USSR

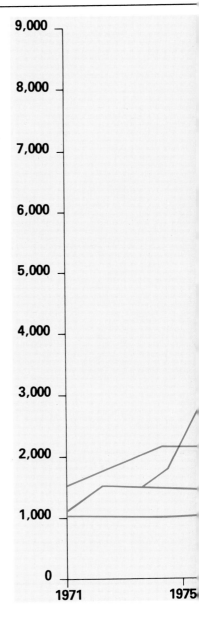

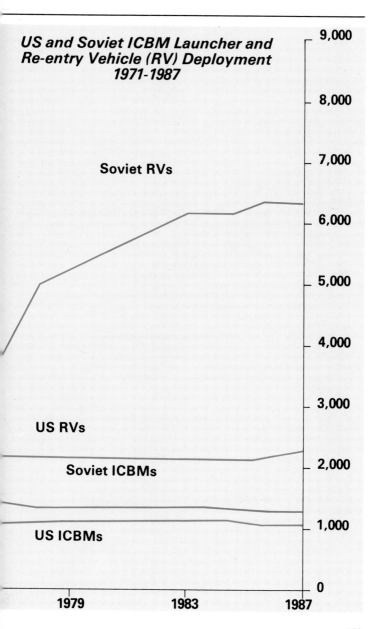

US and Soviet ICBM Launcher and Re-entry Vehicle (RV) Deployment 1971-1987

Soviet RVs

US RVs

Soviet ICBMs

US ICBMs

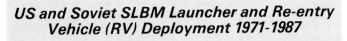

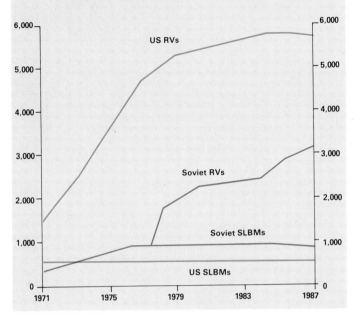

US and Soviet SLBM Launcher and Re-entry Vehicle (RV) Deployment 1971-1987

Above: The Soviets have more SLBMs, the USN more MIRVs.

knows about US intelligence-gathering activities in general, the US obviously does not wish to prejudice particular sources nor do they wish to betray exactly how precise (or, perhaps, imprecise!) some of their intelligence gathering might be. Thus US information on Soviet systems may not always be as precise as might be wished; the problem being, of course, that there is no indication of the degree of accuracy of each item of published information.

Then, having established a set of figures for the systems, the question arises of how to use them and to interpret the results. Tables of weapons totals and of nuclear yields can be compiled, but every question that is answered seems to lead to at least one new question. How, for example, can the Soviet SS-18 be related to the US Minuteman ICBM — or to the Poseidon SLBM? The purpose of this section is to try to answer some of these questions and

TABLE 1: The Static Balance

System	USA Launchers Deployed	Warheads Launche
ICBM		
Minuteman II	442	1
Minuteman III	536	3
Peacekeeper	14	10
Sub-Total ICBM	992	
SLBM		
Poseidon C-3	256	10
Trident I C-4	384	8
Sub-Total SLBM	640	
BOMBERS		
B-52G/H (non-ALCM)	98	12
B-52G/H (ALCM)	46	12
B-1B	19	32
Sub-Total Bombers	163	
TOTALS	1,795	

to endeavour to place the strategic weapons of the two Superpowers in some form of relationship the one to the other, in spite of the problems involved.

Systems Included

The first problem is to establish just what is meant by 'strategic'. After much discussion at the SALT II talks, it was finally agreed in the SALT II Treaty, Article II, that, in respect of ICBMs, this was to be a range 'in excess of 5,500 kilometres' (2,970 nautical miles). For SLBMs the definition was 'launchers of ballistic missiles installed on any nuclear-powered submarine or launchers of modern ballistic missiles on any submarine, regardless of its type.' (The expression 'modern' was subsequently clarified to mean a missile deployed after 1965). Thus, there is comparatively little scope for misunderstanding about what constitutes a strategic missile, whether land- or maritime-based, although there has been considerable discussion on the subject of 'modifications'.

For bombers the position is not so clear-cut, since their range can vary dramatically, depending upon flight profile, payload and whether or not in-flight refuelling is possible. Here again, SALT II has helped to clarify most of the issues, by actually listing the aircraft to be categorised as 'strategic', which, at the time SALT II was being negotiated were the B-1 and B-52 for the USA and Tu-95 and Mya-4 for the USSR. In addition, any bomber was deemed to be 'heavy' if it could be equipped with air-to-surface ballistic missiles or cruise missiles capable of ranges in excess of 600km (324nm) which automatically brings in the Soviet Blackjack.

Weapon Numbers

During the operational life of a missile system a variety of modifications will inevitably be made; some will be relatively minor (say, the renewal of the propulsion system), but others may well effect the strategic balance; for example, installing MIRVs on a missile which previously had only a single warhead. Thus, for example, the Soviet Navy's SS-N-18 has been

USA/USSR (December 31 1987)

Total Warheads	System	Launchers Deployed	USSR Warheads per Launcher	Total Warheads
442	S.11	440	1	440
1,608	SS-13	60	1	60
140	SS-17	150	4	600
	SS-18	308	10	3,080
	SS-19	360	6	2,160
	SS-24	—	—	—
	SS-25	72	1	72
2,190		1,390		6,412
2,560	SS-N-6	304	1	304
3,072	SS-N-8	292	1	292
	SS-N-17	12	*1	12
	SS-N-18	224	7	1,568
	SS-N-20	80	9	720
	SS-N-23	32	10	320
5,632		944		3,216
1,176	Bear-H (ALCM)	40	6	240
552	Bear-B/-C/-G	100	4	400
608	Mya-4	20	4	80
2,336		160		720
10,158		2,494		10,348

TABLE 2: Relative Advantages of the Static Balance (USA/USSR)

	USA	USSR	ADVANTAGE
ICBM			
Launcher	992	1,390	USSR 1.4:1
Warhead	2,190	6,412	USSR 2.9:1
SLBM			
Launcher	640	944	USSR 1.5:1
Warhead	5,632	3,216	USA 1.8:1
Bomber			
Launcher	163	160	USA 1:1
Warhead	2,336	720	USA 3.2:1

TABLE 3: The Static Balance: Non-USSR/USSR

NON-USSR				
System	Launchers Deployed	Warheads per Launcher	Total Warheads	System
ICBM				
US	992		2,190	**USSR**
China	20	1	20	
France	18	1	18	
Sub-Total ICBM	1,030		2,228	
SLBM				
US	640		5,632	**USSR**
China	24	1	24	
France				
M-20	80	1	80	
M-4	16	6	96	
UK	64	1	64	
Sub-Total SLBM	824		5,896	
BOMBERS				
USA	163		2,236	**USSR**
PRC	100	1	100	
France	36	1	36	
Sub-Total Bombers	299		2,472	
TOTALS	2,153		10,596	

deployed in three versions. Mod 1 had three 250KT MIRV; Mod 2 had one 450KT warhead; Mod 3 had seven 250KT MIRVs. The existence of these different payloads will be known from observation of tests, but there is no way of knowing which particular version has been deployed and where. However, again in SALT II, it was agreed that where a launcher was developed and tested with a MIRV capability, then all versions of that system would be deemed to be MIRVed.

Calculations become somewhat more complicated when operational loadings are to be taken into account.

For example, MIRVed ICBMs and SLBMs can carry their maximum number of MIRVs over a specific range. If they are required to fly greater distances, then the payload, ie, the number of MIRVs, must be reduced. Further, if a specific mission requires extra penaids or decoys then this will most probably have to be done at the expense of MIRVs.

With bombers the situation is more complicated still, since not only can payload be traded against fuel, but there are permutations within the payload, too, depending upon the mission the aircraft is required to fulfill. For example, the B-52 can carry a

TABLE 4: Relative Advantages of the Static Balance Non-USSR/USSR

	Non-USSR	USSR	ADVANTAGE
ICBM			
Launcher	1,030	1,390	USSR 1.35:1
Warhead	2,228	6,412	USSR 2.88:1
SLBM			
Launcher	824	944	USSR 1.15:1
Warhead	5,896	3,216	Non-USSR 2.15:1
Bomber			
Launcher	299	160	Non-USSR 1.87:1
Warhead	2,472	720	Non-USSR 3.43:1

(December 31 1987)

USSR

Launchers Deployed	Warheads per Launcher	Total Warheads
1,390		6,412
1,390		6,412
944		3,216
944		3,216
160		720
160		720
2,494		10,345

worth exploring further. Table 2, for example, shows that the static balance between the two Superpowers gives relative advantages, some to the USA and some to the USSR.

However, the USSR has long argued that all nuclear weapons that can strike the territory of either side should be included. In their case, this means that their opponents' total should include the nuclear weapons of China, France and the UK, as well as US forward-based weapons like Pershing 2. If the question of forward-based US systems is ignored and the strategic nuclear arms of other nations are included then Table 3 is the result.

The relative advantages of Table 4 do not dramatically change the overall situation, and certainly do not tip the balance from one 'side' to another. As the non-Soviet powers deploy more of the new SLBMs, however, all with MIRVs, the balance of warheads in that particular field will swing even further against the USSR. As always with statistics they do not show that the USSR is compelled to look to five potentially hostile powers possessing strategic weapons, whereas those four powers themselves only have to look to one possible aggressor. This problem for the USSR is exacerbated in that for a variety of political reasons those four powers would not necessarily act in concert and might well use different criteria for deciding upon nuclear release. In other words, if the USSR was engaged in the early stages of a nuclear war with the USA, could it afford to ignore a potential threat from China?

variety of combinations of SRAM, ALCM and gravity bombs; for a penetration role it would carry gravity bombs and possibly a few SRAM, whereas for a stand-off mission it would carry ALCM and, possibly, a few SRAM.

The Strategic Balance

Table 1 shows the static balance, as of 1987. Static balances take account simply of the estimated numbers of launchers and warheads, and the current convention is to use the SALT II counting rules. Table 1 is, however, based upon a number of assumptions, some of which are

Effective Megatonnage/ Reliability

The assessment so far takes no account of the relative value of the weapons themselves. They are designed, essentially, with two requirements in mind: firstly, for attacks against large area targets such as cities, and secondly for attacks against smaller areas, such as missile silos, that will almost certainly have been given some protective 'hardening'.

Those nuclear weapons that are least accurate are naturally the ones used against the 'soft' area targets. The various weapons of this type available to either side are normally compared in terms of their Effective Megatonnage (EMT). The mathematical equations used to define this, by taking into account accuracy, size of warhead and the height at which the nuclear bomb is detonated, are shown in the glossary.

Known as Counter-Value Weapons because they are essentially deployed as a deterrent, to warn an enemy that they can cause his homeland great harm if he attacks (as opposed to the Counter-Force Weapons that can strike directly at an enemy's nuclear arsenal), these armaments are normally compared as in Table 5, and this comparison demonstrates that whereas the USSR has a 1.8:1 advantage in launchers, this reduces to virtual parity in warheads but increases to 2.6:1 in Effective Megatonnage. In effect, each side could attack roughly the same number of targets, but the USSR could expect to inflict twice as much damage. Two systems — the SS-N-18 and the SS-N-19 — afford the USSR this advantage in the Effective Megatonnage comparison.

Counter-Military Potential

The ability of a missile force to attack hard targets (its Counter-Military

TABLE 5: Effective Megaton

System	Launchers Deployed
Minuteman II	442
Poseidon C-3	256
Trident C-4	384
TOTAL USA	1,082
SS-N-6	304
SS-N-8	292
SS-N-17	12
SS-N-18	224
SS-N-20	80
SS-N-23	32
SS-11	440
SS-13	60
SS-17	150
SS-19	360
TOTAL USSR	1,954

Above: Effective Megatonnage (EMT) enables counter-value weapons to be compared. This

TABLE 6: Possible USA/USSI

System	Launchers Deployed
Minuteman II	442
Minuteman III	536
Peacekeeper	14
US ICBMs	992
SS-11	440
SS-12	60
SS-17	150
SS-18	308
SS-19	360
SS-25	72
USSR ICBMs	1,390

Above: Possible ICBM availability budgets based on the following assumed availabilities: fielded since 1982 = 95 per cent;

of USA and USSR Counter-value Weapons

Warheads per Launcher	Total Warheads	Raw Yield Per Warhead	EMT Per Warhead	Total EMT
1	442	1.2MT	1.095	484
10	2,560	0.04MT	0.117	300
8	3,072	0.1MT	0.215	660
	6,074			1,444
1	304	0.35	0.497	151
1	292	0.8	0.86	251
1	12	0.5	0.63	8
7	1,568	0.2	0.34	533
6	480	0.1	0.215	103
10	320	0.35	0.497	159
3	1,320	0.25	0.397	524
1	60	0.6	0.71	43
4	600	0.75	0.825	945
6	2.160	0.55	0.671	1,450
	7,116			3,717

table shows that in this weapon category, the USSR has almost double the launchers of the USA but that in individual warheads there is virtual parity between the two sides.

CBM Availability

Date fielded	Availability		Warheads Per Launcher	Availability Number
	Percent	Number		
	USA			
1966	85	375	1	375
1970	85	456	3	1,368
1987	95	13	10	130
		844		1,873
	USSR			
1966	85	374	1	374
1972	85	51	1	51
1979	90	135	4	540
1979	90	277	10	2,770
1979	90	324	6	1,944
1985	95	68	1	68
		1,229		5,747

fielded since 1977 = 90 per cent; systems fielded earlier = 85 per cent. Availability also depends upon the strategy employed. For instance, re-targeting may add or subtract warheads which in turn affects serviceability of the system.

Potential — CMP) depends upon characteristics different to those required for soft targets. The relationship between yield (the power of the weapon) and precision is critical. Again, in the glossary the mathematical equations are described. In making these calculations it becomes clear that if the yield is doubled but the accuracy remains unchanged, then the CMP increases by just 1.56. However, if the accuracy is doubled and the yield remains the same, CMP goes up four times. Accuracy is thus the key to increasing CMP.

Reliability

Availability is the expression of whether or not a weapons system will be 'ready-to-go' at the moment it is required; reliability is an assessment of the probability that it will actually work from the moment of giving it the instruction to go, through its flight, to its arrival at the target. Whether or not it destroys a hard target must then be assessed separately; a function termed the 'kill probability'.

The general approach to determining the probability of success for a complex operation such as the flight of an ICBM, is to break it down into a sequence of independent events. Having done this the next step is to determine the probability of the occurence of each event. Then, multiplying these probabilities together gives the overall probability of success — a figure giving an indication that the missile in question will successfully accomplish its mission.

TABLE 7: Possible USA/USSR

Missile	SSBN Type	Fleet Total
Poseidon	Lafayette/ Franklin	12
Trident	Lafayette/ Franklin	12
	Ohio	8
TOTAL USA		**30**
SS-N-6	Yankee I	21
S-N-8	Golf III	1
	Hotel III	
	Delta I	18
	Delta II	4
SS-N-17	Yankee II	1
SS-N-18	Delta III	14
SS-N-20	Typhoon	4
SS-N-23	Delta IV	3
TOTAL USSR		**67**

For a missile to achieve a high probability of success on a complete mission, the probability of success at each stage must be very high. Table 8 gives an indication of how this would be worked out.

Right: Nuclear weapons testing is an important part of improving the quality of warheads and increasing reliability. Today all development and qualification tests take place underground.

TABLE 8: Typical Assessment of Reliability of First RV of Missile System

1st stage motor fires successfully	95 per cent
Missile leaves silo	95 per cent
2nd stage motor fires	98 per cent
2nd stage separation	98 per cent
2nd stage motor terminates correctly	98 per cent
Nose shroud separates	98 per cent
Post-boost vehicle separates	98 per cent
PBV despatches all RVs correctly	95 per cent
RV penetrates atmosphere and arrives on target	90 per cent
Warhead detonates correctly	95 per cent
SYSTEM RELIABILITY	**66 per cent**

SSBN/SLBM Availability

Percentage Availability	Number Available	Launch Tubes	Total Launchers	Less One Tube Per Available SSBN	Warheads per Launcher	Total Warheads
USA						
55	6	16	96	90	14	1,260
55	6	16	96	90	8	720
66	5	24	120	115	8	920
	17		312	295		2,900
USSR						
30	6	16	96	90	1	90
30	1	6	6	5		
30	5	12	60	55	1	75
30	1	16	16	15		
30	1	12	12	11	1	11
30	4	16	64	60	7	320
40	1	20	20	19	9	171
40	1	16	16	15	10	150
	20		290	270		817

Glosssary

(CMP) Counter-Military Potential — An expression of the lethality of a weapon against a hardened target derived from the expression:

$$CMP = \frac{(Yield)^{2/3}}{CEP^+}$$

(CEP) Circular Error Probable — The delivery precision of a weapon system, normally measured in nautical miles or kilometres. It is the radius of a circle, centred upon the mean point of impact, within which 50 percent of the missiles aimed at the target will fall. The mean point of impact will almost always be offset from the centre of the target by the bias (qv). The CEP is normally assessed at the missile's maximum range; at less than the maximum range the CEP reduces in proportion, ie:

$$CEP_{Range\ X} = CEP_{Maximum\ range} \times \frac{Range\ X}{Maximum\ Range}$$

Counter-Value — The employment of strategic forces to attack selected hostile population centres, industries and resources which constitute the essential fabric of the nation.

(EMT) Effective Megatonnage — A measure used to compare the destructive potential of a nuclear warhead against relatively soft 'counter-value' (qv) target. EMT is computed from the expression;

$$EMT = (Yield)^n.$$

[n = 2/3 except where Yield is less than 1MT, when n = 1/2.]

(EMP) Electro-Magnetic Pulse — The very brief, but very powerful pulse of electro-magnetic radiation at radio frequencies produced by a nuclear explosion. The intense electric and magnetic fields will damage electrical and electronic equipment over a large area, unless steps have been taken to give it 'EMP protection.'

Overpressure — The pressure resulting from the blast wave of an explosion. It is used concerning silos to indicate 'hardness'; ie, a '3,000psi silo' is a silo designed to survive undamaged an overpressure of 3,000psi.

(Penaids) Penetration Aids — Devices employed by offensive weapons systems (eg, ballistic missiles, bombers) to increase the probability of penetrating hostile defences. They are frequently designed to simulate or mask an aircraft or ballistic missile warhead in order to mislead hostile radar and/or divert defensive antiaircraft or antimissile fire. (See also 'decoy')

Throw-Weight — The useful weight which is placed on a trajectory toward the target by the boost or main propulsion stages of a missile. For the purposes of SALT II throw-weight was defined as the sum of the weights of:
— the RV or RVs.
— any PBV or similar device for releasing or targeting one or more RVs.
— any anti-ballistic missile penetration aids, including their release devices.

Yield — The energy released in a nuclear explosion, expressed in terms of the equivalent number of tons of TNT releasing the same amount of energy. Normally expressed in terms of thousands of tons of TNT (kilotons) or millions of tons (megatons). The basic of 'TNT equivalence' is that the explosion of 1 ton of TNT is assumed to release 10^6 calories of energy (1KT = 10^{12} calories; 1MT = 10^{15} calories). The yield is manifested as nuclear radiation, thermal radiation, and blast energy, the actual distribution being dependent upon the medium in which the explosion occurs, the type of weapon and the time after detonation.